# MASTERPIECES OF DECLARER PLAY

The title of this book carries a double meaning. Firstly, each of its pages offers a piece of wisdom regarding how to play as declarer. Between these and those contained in the companion book on defence, they capture the essence of the author's extensive knowledge about, and feel for, the game of bridge. Secondly, many of the examples chosen to illustrate the points are classics in themselves. This refreshing collection of hands must surely be one of the most beautiful seen in recent years.

*Masterpieces of Declarer Play* appears as a natural sequel to *The Golden Rules of Declarer Play* (co-written with Marc Smith). Whereas that earlier volume explained the basic principles, this one provides the discerning reader with a deeper insight into the game's strategic aspects.

If at the table you manage to follow all the snippets of advice offered, your game can only improve. Unless you already rank amongst the world's great card players, you are bound to learn something from the tips. Even those now at the top should find the example hands of sufficient interest to make each hour of reading this book worthwhile.

A word of warning – once you start thumbing through the pages you will find it difficult to stop. However, as with a fine wine, the best way to savour this vintage is by sampling a little at a time!

*by Julian Pottage and Marc Smith*

THE GOLDEN RULES OF DEFENCE
THE GOLDEN RULES OF DECLARER PLAY

# MASTERPIECES OF DECLARER PLAY

Julian Pottage

CASSELL&CO
IN ASSOCIATION WITH
PETER CRAWLEY

First published in Great Britain 2001
in association with Peter Crawley
by Cassell & Co
Wellington House, 125 Strand, London WC2R 0BB
an imprint of the Orion Publishing Group Ltd

ISBN 0–304–35791–X

Typeset at The Spartan Press Ltd
Lymington, Hants

Printed and Bound in Great Britain by
Mackays of Chatham, Kent

# Contents

# Standard System Summary

## Natural bidding with 5-card majors and a variable no-trump

Responses: Splinters, limit raises (inverted minors), 2NT Baron
1NT opening 12-14 non-vulnerable, 15-17 vul., responses:

   2♣ Stayman, 2♦, 2♥, 2♠, 2NT transfers, Lebensohl 2NT
   to show weaker hand/interest in other major in competition
2♣ opening strong (may be good Acol Two) with 2♦ negative
2♦, 2♥, 2♠ openers = Weak Twos: 6 suit and 5-9/6-10 points,

   2NT response to these asks for range and suit quality
2NT opening 20-22 with 3♣ Stayman, 3♦, 3♥ transfers
3 & 4 opening of a suit pre-emptive and 3NT opener gambling
Opener's rebid of 1NT wide-range 12-16 with 2♣ enquiry
Fourth-suit forcing sequences can stop in 2NT
Cue-bids: first-round controls first (or king in partner's suit)
4NT Roman Key Card Blackwood: trump king = 5th ace, replies:

   5♣ = 0 or 3, 5♦ = 1 or 4, 5♥ = 2 or 5, 5♠ = 2 or 5 + trump queen
In competition after opening/overcall cue-bid shows value raise
and jumps are pre-emptive, fit-showing jumps in new suits
Jump overcalls weak at all vulnerabilities with 6+ card suit
2NT overcall lowest 2 unbid suits
Cue-bid overcall over 1♣/1♦ = 5/5+ majors weak/strong, over
1♥/1♠ shows 5/5+ other major plus one minor weak/strong
Defence to 1NT: 2♣ = hearts & another, 2♦ = spades & another,
double is penalties over both weak and strong no-trumps
Defence to Weak Twos: take-out double with 2NT Lebensohl
Negative and competitive doubles apply up to 4♦

## Leads and carding methods

Leads: top of sequence or interior sequence (except A-K bare),
4th highest from honour suits, 2nd highest from poor ones
On partner's lead: standard count (rarely high to encourage)
Following suit: standard count if given (i.e., peter = even no.)
Discards are standard count, tend to be in suits not wanted led
Suit preference signals, high card for high suit etc., widely used

# Foreword

May God bless you with plenty of peace and quiet when you read this book. Having two lovely little boys at home whilst I was drafting it, I had to make the most of such moments!

I collected the examples used in this work over a period of some fifteen years. A fair number closely resemble hands I met at the table. In many cases I have made the odd tweak in either the bidding or the cards to make the key point clearer. A further group derives from ideas that I have had or chanced upon. I have tried to present these in an original and apt setting.

You will gain the most benefit if you spend just a few minutes studying each example with only your hand and dummy's in view. That way you can form your own plan and develop your natural approach to dummy play, which you can then employ at the table.

On every hand I have assumed rubber bridge or IMP scoring. Therefore, except perhaps in doubled contracts, you need not concern yourself with overtricks or extra undertricks.

Please scrutinise the summary of system notes on page 6, just as you would if you were playing a long match. Within the body of the book all four players are following this standard. As declarer you need to understand the defenders' actions and know what you have divulged about your hand.

Unless you have a fantastic memory, some of the tips will not sink in straight away. So do pick up the book again and again. Moreover you may discover a fresh angle that way. If you have the time, laying out the deals in cards may make it easier to follow some of the more testing subject matter. Happy reading!

Julian Pottage

September 2001

# Acknowledgments

The author wishes to thank the proof-reading team who include: Maureen Dennison, Andrew Southwell and David Tan. With their multitude of talents they uncovered several very good points.

I am most grateful to my darling wife, Helen, who never once complained about 'just another five minutes writing the book'. My eldest sons, Matthew and Edward, played their part too – they somehow avoided either wrecking the computer or disturbing my working papers!

Peter Crawley and Ron Klinger were helpful as always, coming up with ideas for the book's title and making a number of other most constructive suggestions. Finally I would like to mention William Bailey. His 'Deep Finesse' program proved a godsend in checking the hand analysis.

# 1. Declarer Play at No-Trumps

The full name of our game, contract bridge, implies that one's primary aim is to bid and make a contract. It thus seems natural to consider declarer play before defence, which explains why this book has gone to press a year in advance of *Masterpieces of Defence*.

For two main reasons we shall study no-trump contracts ahead of suit play. Firstly, pretty well every technique you care to employ in trumpless positions will remain valid when ruffing becomes an option. Secondly, except for the strip and throw in, no-trump play is usually simpler.

With no trumps around, cards that look like winners tend to take tricks. Moreover, those that seem to be losers rarely score. The fact that you cannot interrupt the run of the enemy's suit with a ruff often assumes prime importance. This means that many no-trump contracts turn into a race between declarer and the defenders. Each side strives to set up and run their own long suit before the enemy exploits theirs.

Most of the time declarer and dummy combined possess the lion's share of the high cards. Therefore their honours mesh together and entries are less often a problem for them. On the other hand, the defence makes the opening lead, which gives them a head start. This all leads to some exciting battles . . .

Example 1

Love All
Dealer East

♠ Q J 9
♡ Q J 3 2
◇ K J
♣ K 10 6 2

| SOUTH | WEST | NORTH | EAST |
|-------|------|-------|------|
|       |      |       | Pass |
| 1NT   | Pass | 3NT   | End  |

N
W E
S

♠ 10 8 6 4 3
♡ A 5
◇ A 6 2
♣ A 9 4

With such poor spades you open a weak no-trump. Partner, holding many soft values, dispenses with Stayman and raises to game. West leads the seven of hearts, which will be second or fourth highest if it comes from length.

How do you plan the play?

Example 2

East–West game
Dealer South

♠ A K J
♡ 6 3
◇ A J 6 4 3
♣ 6 5 2

| SOUTH | WEST | NORTH | EAST |
|-------|------|-------|------|
| 1NT   | Pass | 3NT   | End  |

N
W E
S

♠ 9 4 3
♡ A J
◇ K 8 2
♣ A 10 8 4 3

After a very similar auction West leads the six of spades.
What assessment do you make of this hand?

Example 3

♠ A K J 7 6 5
♡ K 7

North–South game
Dealer North

♢ 7 4
♣ A 7 5

| SOUTH | WEST | NORTH | EAST |
|-------|------|-------|------|
|       |      | 1♠    | Pass |
| 3♣    | Pass | 3♠    | Pass |
| 3NT   | All Pass |   |      |

```
        N
    W       E
        S
```

♠ 3
♡ A Q 8
♢ K 10 8 6
♣ Q J 10 9 2

You conduct a natural sequence to 3NT. West leads the five of diamonds and East puts up the jack.

How do you plan the play?

Example 4

♠ K 8 2
♡ 9 5 2

East–West game
Dealer South

♢ J 10 6 5 3 2
♣ 9

| SOUTH | WEST | NORTH | EAST |
|-------|------|-------|------|
| 2♣    | Pass | 2♢    | Pass |
| 2NT   | Pass | 3NT   | End  |

```
        N
    W       E
        S
```

♠ A Q 4
♡ A K 3
♢ A 7
♣ K Q J 4 3

West leads the queen of hearts and East plays the eight, suggesting an even number.

How can you make the most of your chances?

12

Example 1

```
              ♠ Q J 9
              ♡ Q J 3 2
              ◇ K J
              ♣ K 10 6 2

  ♠ K 5 2        N        ♠ A 7
  ♡ 7 4      W       E    ♡ K 10 9 8 6
  ◇ 9 8 5 4               ◇ Q 10 7 3
  ♣ Q 8 7 5      S        ♣ J 3

              ♠ 10 8 6 4 3
              ♡ A 5
              ◇ A 6 2
              ♣ A 9 4
```

After a simple sequence you reach 3NT and West leads the seven of hearts.

A quick inspection reveals that, given time, you will have enough winners by setting up the spades. Even if the diamond finesse is wrong you can make three spades, two hearts, two diamonds and two clubs. So you address the possible danger of the defenders scoring five tricks first.

If the king of hearts lies on your left, you are okay as you will have the hearts trebly stopped. A good player would realise that nobody leads the seven from ♡10-9-8-7-x and perhaps go no further. You should in addition consider whether West might have begun with a doubleton heart. Then West will want to win the first spade and clear the hearts whilst East retains a spade entry. How do you thwart this?

You toy with the idea of allowing the seven of hearts to hold. The problem is that a diamond switch through the king-jack in dummy could then prove awkward. Instead you should play North's queen of hearts at trick one, as seems the natural thing to do, but duck East's king. By this means you can establish your spades before your second heart stopper has gone. True, you would still go down if East held five hearts and both spade entries, but then there is not much you can do about that.

*Good defenders often lead from a short suit if they hold few values – stay alert to this.*

Example 2

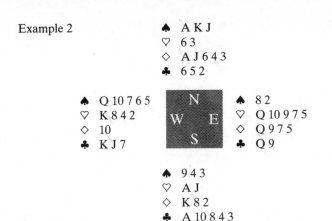

```
                        ♠ A K J
                        ♡ 6 3
                        ◇ A J 6 4 3
                        ♣ 6 5 2

    ♠ Q 10 7 6 5                        ♠ 8 2
    ♡ K 8 4 2                           ♡ Q 10 9 7 5
    ◇ 10                                ◇ Q 9 7 5
    ♣ K J 7                             ♣ Q 9

                        ♠ 9 4 3
                        ♡ A J
                        ◇ K 8 2
                        ♣ A 10 8 4 3
```

West leads the six of spades against your 3NT.

You may give this contract a healthy prognosis. Although you can count on only six certain winners, dummy contains an attractive five-card suit. If the diamonds break 3-2 with the queen onside, you can come to five tricks in that suit easily enough. A less helpful diamond position may also suffice. A 4-1 split with the finesse right, or 3-2 but the queen wrong, or a bare queen anywhere would each allow you four tricks. You would then simply need the spades to yield three winners. Can you see an extra chance?

The eight of diamonds in your hand means that you might be able to cater for queen to four diamonds with East. If you know that you require just four tricks in the suit, you can cash the ace and play back to the eight. This works wonders when West holds a lone nine or ten. Therefore you should finesse the jack of spades at trick one. When this holds you take the safety play in diamonds to ensure your nine tricks.

Note that many declarers would win the first trick with a top spade for fear of a heart switch. Of course such a concern is ill founded. If East possesses the queen of spades, you need five diamond tricks for the contract, so you do not expect to lose the lead twice.

***If a key suit offers a safety option, aim to find out how many tricks you need in the suit before tackling it.***

Example 3

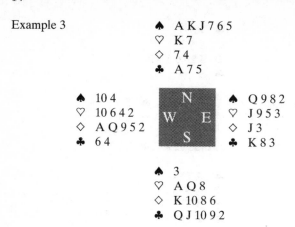

```
              ♠ A K J 7 6 5
              ♡ K 7
              ◇ 7 4
              ♣ A 7 5

♠ 10 4           N           ♠ Q 9 8 2
♡ 10 6 4 2    W     E        ♡ J 9 5 3
◇ A Q 9 5 2                  ◇ J 3
♣ 6 4            S           ♣ K 8 3

              ♠ 3
              ♡ A Q 8
              ◇ K 10 8 6
              ♣ Q J 10 9 2
```

You are in 3NT once more. West leads the five of diamonds and East puts up the jack.

Prospects look rosy. You have seven tricks readily on tap, and you hold a long suit in each hand. Indeed your high quality clubs should provide ample extra winners. Hence you assess whether the defence might cash five tricks before the clubs run.

If West has led from a short suit, you are home and dry. West may also have begun with six diamonds or ◇A-Q-9-5-3, ◇A-Q-9-5-2, or ◇A-Q-9-5. In the first case you have nothing to worry about as East cannot return the suit. Conversely, if West started off with five diamonds and East gains the lead, they could beat you. Remember, any black-suit finesse will go into the hand on your right. Perhaps you consider starting on clubs with the ace, but the king is unlikely to fall. Maybe withholding your king of diamonds will help . . .

Yes, ducking trick one will work when the diamonds split 5-2, even if you lose your king. Try it and see. The defenders score the jack, queen and ace but West has no side entry and they wind up with only three diamond tricks. Since there are two ways West can have five diamonds to just one of having four, holding up must be the correct play. You may spot an added reason for assuming the lead comes from five: with a four-card suit headed by a tenace, West might have led something else.

***Sometimes you can work out all the relevant defensive holdings – when you get such a chance, take it.***

Example 4

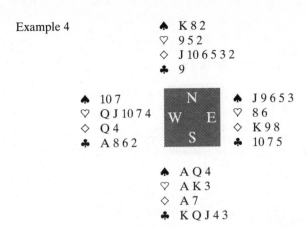

&spades; K 8 2
&hearts; 9 5 2
&diams; J 10 6 5 3 2
&clubs; 9

&spades; 10 7
&hearts; Q J 10 7 4
&diams; Q 4
&clubs; A 8 6 2

&spades; J 9 6 5 3
&hearts; 8 6
&diams; K 9 8
&clubs; 10 7 5

&spades; A Q 4
&hearts; A K 3
&diams; A 7
&clubs; K Q J 4 3

Once more you cruise into the no-trump game. West leads the queen of hearts and East plays the eight, suggesting an even number.

The entry position renders dummy's long diamonds useless. Unless one defender holds something like king-queen tight, you cannot develop the suit. This means you need to play on clubs even though you require them to divide 4-3 and expect to give up the lead twice. Thus, as is often the case, the suit attacked by the defence at trick one represents a threat. We now turn to that.

You can duck the first heart and win the second. So only if West obtains the lead twice will too many hearts be run against you. How can you minimise the risk of West winning two clubs?

West must get in twice with &clubs;A-10-x-x and should not do so if East has the club ace (if East wins a club and shifts to a low diamond, you will rise with the ace, hoping to block the suit). The two key holdings for West are &clubs;A-10-x, which gives East &clubs;x-x-x-x, and &clubs;A-x-x-x, leaving East with &clubs;10-x-x. In the first case you must lay down a high club and concede the fourth round to East. In the latter, you want to lead to the nine, forcing East to win the first club trick. There are ten ways West can have the former holding, but just five of the second. This marks your correct play. Win the second heart and lead a low club. You win any return and clear the clubs.

**_When only one opponent can harm you, look for a way to lose the lead to the other defender._**

Example 5

♠ 9 7 6 4
♡ J 7 3 2

North–South game
Dealer South

◇ 10 4 3
♣ A K

| SOUTH | WEST | NORTH | EAST |
|-------|------|-------|------|
| 1◇ | Pass | 1♡ | Pass |
| 2♣ | Pass | 2◇ | Pass |
| 2NT | Pass | 3NT | End |

♠ A 2
♡ A 9
◇ A K 7 6 2
♣ Q 9 3 2

West leads the five of spades and East contributes the king. What are your plans, both for this trick and later?

Example 6

♠ 10 9 2
♡ A J

East–West game
Dealer North

◇ 4 2
♣ A 10 9 8 5 2

| SOUTH | WEST | NORTH | EAST |
|-------|------|-------|------|
| | | Pass | 1♡ |
| 1NT | Pass | 3NT | End |

♠ Q J 7 6
♡ K 8 5
◇ A Q 10 3
♣ K Q

West leads the six of hearts, covered by North's jack and East's queen.

How do you intend to score at least nine tricks?

Example 7

♠ A 9 5
♡ A Q

East–West game
Dealer North

♢ A Q 5 2
♣ K 7 6 2

| SOUTH | WEST | NORTH | EAST |
|-------|------|-------|------|
|       |      | 1♢    | Pass |
| 1NT   | Pass | 3NT   | End  |

♠ 10 3
♡ 10 8 5
♢ K J 4
♣ A 9 8 5 3

West leads the six of spades, you play low from dummy and East's jack wins. The queen of spades comes straight back, West following downwards with the two.

How do you plan the play from here?

Example 8

♠ 10 3
♡ 9 2

Love All
Dealer North

♢ K 8 3
♣ Q J 10 5 4 2

| SOUTH | WEST | NORTH | EAST |
|-------|------|-------|------|
|       |      | Pass  | 3♢   |
| 3NT   | All Pass |    |      |

♠ A K 6 5 4
♡ A 7 5
♢ Q 10 5
♣ A K

West leads the heart king and East plays the three, showing an odd number. You decide to hold up twice and East follows to the second and third round of hearts. Now you have to take your ace, throwing a spade from dummy.

How do you proceed?

Example 5

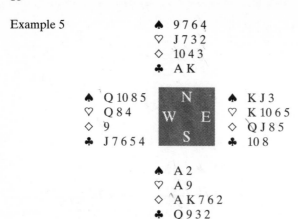

♠ 9 7 6 4
♡ J 7 3 2
◇ 10 4 3
♣ A K

♠ Q 10 8 5
♡ Q 8 4
◇ 9
♣ J 7 6 5 4

♠ K J 3
♡ K 10 6 5
◇ Q J 8 5
♣ 10 8

♠ A 2
♡ A 9
◇ A K 7 6 2
♣ Q 9 3 2

With the enemy silent you reach 3NT. West leads the five of spades and East contributes the king.

You cannot tell how the spade suit splits, nor do you care. Holding ♠Q-J-10-x-x West would no doubt have led an honour. So you capture the king with your ace, knowing dummy's nine will block the suit if it breaks 5-2. This way you sidestep the danger of a heart switch through your doubleton ace. With that hurdle over, you figure out how best to set up your diamonds.

As a 3-2 diamond split makes the contract a cinch, imagine they break 4-1. Suppose you cash a top diamond and a lone honour falls on your right. You can continue with a low one, but what happens then? West rises with the other diamond picture and cashes some spades. Afterwards the defence can shift to hearts, driving out your ace. North's now bare ten of diamonds and ace-king of clubs will leave you stranded on the table.

You should focus rather on a singleton diamond with West, which will need to be the eight or nine. You *could* start with a low card from hand and take two finesses against East, but then you would go down on some 3-2 breaks. The correct play is to cross over with a club and lead the diamond ten. If East plays an honour, go back to the table with a second club and lead the three of diamonds, covering East's card.

***Before you make a play, consider whether you have the entries to bring off what you are trying to achieve.***

Example 6

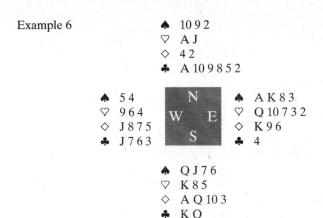

```
              ♠  10 9 2
              ♡  A J
              ◇  4 2
              ♣  A 10 9 8 5 2

  ♠  5 4                        ♠  A K 8 3
  ♡  9 6 4          N           ♡  Q 10 7 3 2
  ◇  J 8 7 5     W     E        ◇  K 9 6
  ♣  J 7 6 3        S           ♣  4

              ♠  Q J 7 6
              ♡  K 8 5
              ◇  A Q 10 3
              ♣  K Q
```

You steam into 3NT after East has opened 1♡ second in hand. West leads the six of hearts, covered by North's jack and East's queen.

Since dummy's ace of hearts may provide a vital entry to the long clubs, you will have to take your king of hearts. That gets one thing to think of out of the way.

If you count three tricks outside clubs (two hearts and one diamond) then you will want to play the clubs for six tricks. In consequence you will cash the king-queen from your hand and then cross over to dummy. A glance at the diagram reveals that such a line fails – could you have foreseen this?

There are 26 high card points in the two hands you can see. You also know that East has a hand good enough to open the bidding in second seat vulnerable against not. From this you can infer the diamond finesse is almost a certainty.

Assuming you make two diamonds, you need only five club winners. So overtake the second round with the ace and clear the suit. You thereby guarantee five club tricks and can take the diamond finesse after cashing them. Note that if West has the ◇K, East rates to hold at least ten major suit cards to justify an opening bid. In that case West probably has ♣J-x-x-x anyway.

***In assessing your likely winners, make sure you take into account all the facts known to you.***

Example 7

```
              ♠  A 9 5
              ♡  A Q
              ◇  A Q 5 2
              ♣  K 7 6 2

♠  K 8 7 6 2        N          ♠  Q J 4
♡  J 2                         ♡  K 9 7 6 4 3
◇  10 8 7      W        E      ◇  9 6 3
♣  Q J 4            S          ♣  10

              ♠  10 3
              ♡  10 8 5
              ◇  K J 4
              ♣  A 9 8 5 3
```

Once more partner has put you in Three No-Trumps. West leads the six of spades, you play low from dummy and East's jack wins. The queen of spades comes straight back, West following with the two.

You start by reading the spade position. East's return of a high card and West's second round two both indicate the same thing: the suit is splitting 5-3. So you should again hold up North's ace of spades. When West perseveres with a third spade, you must discard something from hand. Perhaps your possible sources of a ninth trick will affect your choice.

Having exhausted East of spades, you can safely concede a club if one of two things happens. The first is if you lead a club off dummy and the queen comes up on the first round. The other is if you find any three clubs on your right. When in fact East turns up with singleton ten, hearts will have to furnish your game-going trick. Since the heart finesse goes into the East hand, you will remain alive even if it fails. What hope would you then have?

Aha! Once clubs misbehave and you find the king of hearts offside, you need to rely on the ♡J dropping in two rounds. Provided you have kept all your hearts, you will then make your ten. The conclusion is that you should release a club at trick three – this can only ever cost an overtrick, not the contract.

***Prior to making a discard, check the potential value of the card you plan to let go.***

Example 8

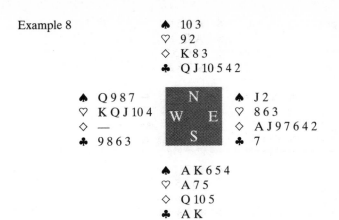

♠ 10 3
♡ 9 2
◇ K 8 3
♣ Q J 10 5 4 2

♠ Q 9 8 7
♡ K Q J 10 4
◇ —
♣ 9 8 6 3

♠ J 2
♡ 8 6 3
◇ A J 9 7 6 4 2
♣ 7

♠ A K 6 5 4
♡ A 7 5
◇ Q 10 5
♣ A K

Upon hearing East open a pre-empt in diamonds, you punt 3NT. West leads the king of hearts and East plays the three, showing an odd number.

Deciding you want to sever the link between the defenders and to learn more about their hands, you hold up twice. East follows to the second and third round of hearts. Now you have to take your ace, throwing a spade from dummy.

Nine prospective winners continue to stare you in the face, but you may still see no means of enjoying North's share of them. Perhaps your spade suit can help . . .

Sadly, even if you could set up two long spades without letting West in, that would put you on course for only eight tricks. Instead you should concentrate on ensuring that East cannot stop you reaching dummy's clubs.

Certainly you can proceed to cash your top cards in the black suits, pitching one club from dummy. This should reduce East to just diamonds. The issue then boils down to one of tackling that suit the correct way. If you lead either the queen or the ten, East will duck. By the same token the ace will appear if you start low to the king. So, what option does that leave you?

Eureka! If you overtake the five with the eight, East can win cheaply but must then lead up to dummy's king.

**Remain calm when you seem to need a miracle – if you focus your energy correctly, a solution may hit you.**

Example 9

Game All
Dealer West

♠ A K 2
♡ A K 9
◇ A J 4
♣ A 7 5 3

| SOUTH | WEST | NORTH | EAST |
|-------|------|--------|------|
|       | 2♡   | Double | Pass |
| 2NT   | Pass | 3NT    | End  |

N
W   E
S

♠ 8 6 5 4
♡ 7 3
◇ K 10 8 6 2
♣ 10 2

West's 2♡ showed 6-10 points with a six-card heart suit. 2NT was Lebensohl, asking North to bid 3♣ so you could sign off in 3◇. Partner was too strong to obey your request!

West leads the queen of hearts.

What layout might give you cause for thought?

Example 10

East–West game
Dealer North

♠ J 5
♡ A
◇ K Q 10 9 8 7 5
♣ A 5 3

| SOUTH | WEST | NORTH | EAST |
|-------|------|-------|------|
|       |      | 1◇    | Pass |
| 1♠    | Pass | 3◇    | Pass |
| 3NT   | All Pass |    |      |

N
W   E
S

♠ A 10 6 4
♡ K Q 2
◇ 4 3
♣ K 7 6 2

West leads the jack of hearts, won perforce by dummy's ace, East playing the eight.

What should your next move be?

**Example 11**

♠ 6 2
♡ A 8 3

North–South game
Dealer South

♦ K Q J 5 4
♣ 8 4 2

| SOUTH | WEST | NORTH | EAST |
|-------|------|-------|------|
| 1NT | Pass | 3NT | End |

♠ A K 9 4
♡ K Q 10
♦ 8 2
♣ A 7 6 5

West leads the king of clubs, which you duck, whilst East plays the three. West continues with the jack on which East pitches the ♡2. There is no point holding up again and also a spade shift may prove awkward, so you win the second club.

How do you aim to find eight more tricks?

**Example 12**

♠ 10
♡ K 10 5

Game All
Dealer South

♦ A Q 10 6 3
♣ 9 8 6 3

| SOUTH | WEST | NORTH | EAST |
|-------|------|-------|------|
| 1NT | Pass | 3NT | End |

♠ A Q J
♡ J 8 4
♦ J 9 8 2
♣ A K 5

West leads the three of spades to North's ten, East's seven and your queen.

How do you approach this hand?

Example 9

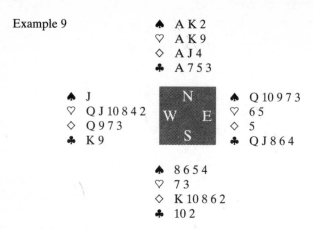

```
            ♠ A K 2
            ♡ A K 9
            ◇ A J 4
            ♣ A 7 5 3

♠ J                        ♠ Q 10 9 7 3
♡ Q J 10 8 4 2     N       ♡ 6 5
◇ Q 9 7 3       W     E    ◇ 5
♣ K 9              S       ♣ Q J 8 6 4

            ♠ 8 6 5 4
            ♡ 7 3
            ◇ K 10 8 6 2
            ♣ 10 2
```

After the Lebensohl convention has made you declarer in 3NT, West (who opened a weak 2♡) leads the queen of hearts.

Outside of diamonds you see five top winners. This means that your main suit merely needs to supply four tricks.

Any time the diamonds are 3-2, they must yield four tricks even with the finesse wrong. If East has four diamonds, you will fare better still. You cash the ace, lead the jack forcing a cover, and return to dummy to finesse the eight. You thus conclude that only if West holds four diamonds might a problem arise. West will then allow dummy's jack to win the second round of the suit, thereby limiting you to three easy tricks.

You could next try for spades 3-3 but, given red-suit lengths on your left, that rather defies the odds. Provided you won the first trick, you might elect to cash North's tops and exit with a heart. This will produce an endplay if West began with 2-6-4-1 shape. Can we improve on this?

Yes, after taking the first three tricks with the ace of hearts, and the ace and jack of diamonds, duck a club at trick four. You win the heart return and then play off dummy's remaining high card winners. West, who has to keep the ◇Q guarded, can retain only three winning hearts. This allows you to exit with a heart and secure a diamond lead into your king-ten.

***Stripping the hand at no-trumps is often tricky – try to maximise your chance of removing a defender's exit cards.***

Example 10

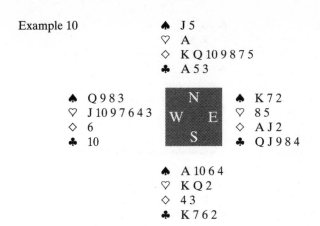

```
              ♠  J 5
              ♡  A
              ◇  K Q 10 9 8 7 5
              ♣  A 5 3

♠ Q 9 8 3           N           ♠  K 7 2
♡ J 10 9 7 6 4 3              ♡  8 5
◇ 6          W         E      ◇  A J 2
♣ 10                S         ♣  Q J 9 8 4

              ♠  A 10 6 4
              ♡  K Q 2
              ◇  4 3
              ♣  K 7 6 2
```

Yet again you arrive in 3NT. West leads the jack of hearts, won perforce by dummy's ace, East playing the eight.

What you do at trick two will depend upon how you intend to handle the diamonds. As a result, we focus on that suit first.

Suppose you lead small from hand to dummy's king. Oh no! If East has ace-jack-other and ducks, dummy's diamonds will be dead. Does inserting the ten work any better?

Yes, unless East has all four diamonds, a first round finesse of the ten will serve your purpose. How then might you cross to the closed hand to start on the diamonds?

If you come over with a spade and West has honour to four, you could lose three spade tricks. East might get in, cash a high spade and continue the suit through your ten to give West two spade tricks. Two diamond losers added to three spades would defeat you. Perhaps it seems safer to use the king of clubs to enter the South hand. Sadly, the way the cards lie, this play fails too. East, who holds a five-card club suit and two diamond entries, will get to score five tricks in the minors.

Since you can afford to lose two diamonds, forget about leading them from hand. Simply call for the ten of diamonds at trick two. You are all right even if someone makes a bare jack.

***Take care about crossing from one hand to the other because you may open up a can of worms by so doing.***

Example 11

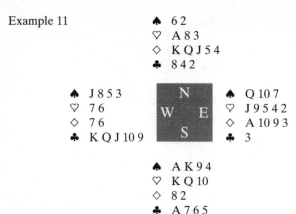

- ♠ 6 2
- ♡ A 8 3
- ◇ K Q J 5 4
- ♣ 8 4 2

West:
- ♠ J 8 5 3
- ♡ 7 6
- ◇ 7 6
- ♣ K Q J 10 9

East:
- ♠ Q 10 7
- ♡ J 9 5 4 2
- ◇ A 10 9 3
- ♣ 3

South:
- ♠ A K 9 4
- ♡ K Q 10
- ◇ 8 2
- ♣ A 7 6 5

Having shown 15-17 balanced you sail into 3NT. West leads the king of clubs, which you duck, while East plays the three. West continues with the jack of clubs on which East pitches the ♡2. You win the second round of clubs with your ace.

Apart from the club already made you have five fast winners: two spades and three hearts. Clearly only dummy's diamonds can make good the deficit. Indeed they may provide four tricks on a 3-3 split. So maybe you can handle some 4-2 breaks.

You require East to hold the ace of diamonds because West has clubs to cash. The problem is that if you lead to an honour, East can withhold the ace. You will then lack the entries to score more than two diamond winners. On the other hand, if you duck the first diamond completely, East may manage to get under West's card. The clubs could then be run against you.

Assuming that West would tend to peter with a doubleton, you cannot cater for either ◇10-x or ◇9-x on your left. Happily you can deal with the actual position. Lead the diamond eight, planning to run it if West does not cover.

Voila! Not only do you keep West off play, but you also force East to win the first diamond. You can then win any return in hand before going on to set up and enjoy the diamonds.

**_With a choice of two cards to lead, neither of which can take a trick, consider the merits of leading the higher one._**

Example 12

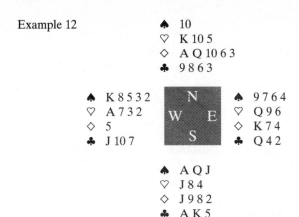

```
                    ♠ 10
                    ♡ K 10 5
                    ◇ A Q 10 6 3
                    ♣ 9 8 6 3

    ♠ K 8 5 3 2         N          ♠ 9 7 6 4
    ♡ A 7 3 2       W       E      ♡ Q 9 6
    ◇ 5                 S          ◇ K 7 4
    ♣ J 10 7                       ♣ Q 4 2

                    ♠ A Q J
                    ♡ J 8 4
                    ◇ J 9 8 2
                    ♣ A K 5
```

Another strong no-trump opener leaves you at the helm in 3NT. West leads the three of spades to North's ten, East's seven and your queen.

Counting four tricks outside dummy's long suit, you realise a successful finesse in it would be just what the doctor ordered. Let us suppose for now that straight after winning the first trick, you run the jack of diamonds to East's king. No doubt a spade will come back through your tenace and you will forlornly try the jack. West will capture this with the king and clear the spades. As the play to trick one has ruled out six spades on your left, you will then go down no matter how well the other suits lie.

Yes, at trick three you could hope West began with three spades. In that case you would rise with the ace to block the suit. Thereafter you would simply need to find West with one or both missing heart honours. However, this is surely a long shot.

Rather than rushing into diamonds, you should aim to secure an early heart trick. As we worked out above, allowing East to get in early would spell defeat. So you must play West for the heart ace rather than the queen. True, West might have ace doubleton heart and clear that suit while East retains the king of diamonds entry. Then again, if the cards happen to sit that way, taking the diamond finesse first would not work either.

**A king-jack type position does not present a true guess if you can ill afford to lose the lead to one defender.**

28

Example 13      ♠ Q J 6
                 ♡ A J
Love All         ◇ K 10 6 5
Dealer South     ♣ Q J 10 7

| SOUTH | WEST | NORTH | EAST |
|-------|------|-------|------|
| 1NT | Pass | 3NT | End |

♠ A K 10
♡ Q 8 5 2
◇ Q J 3
♣ 9 6 4

West leads the four of hearts, won by North's jack as East plays the three.

Plan the play.

Example 14      ♠ 9 4
                 ♡ J 10 4 3
North–South game   ◇ K 8 4 2
Dealer South     ♣ 8 6 2

| SOUTH | WEST | NORTH | EAST |
|-------|------|-------|------|
| 2♣ | Pass | 2◇ | Pass |
| 2NT | Pass | 3♣ | Pass |
| 3♠ | Pass | 3NT | End |

♠ A K Q 3
♡ A 6
◇ Q 6 5 3
♣ A K Q

You are using Stayman after 2NT sequences, so you have shown four spades and denied four hearts.

West leads the three of clubs to East's ten and your king.

What is your strategy for taking eight more tricks?

Example 15

North–South game
Dealer South

♠ A 9
♡ Q 7 4
◇ A K J 9 4
♣ 7 5 4

| SOUTH | WEST | NORTH | EAST |
|-------|------|-------|------|
| 1♣ | Pass | 1◇ | Pass |
| 1NT | Pass | 3NT | End |

♠ Q 8 3
♡ K 9 5 2
◇ 3 2
♣ A K 8 6

West leads the five of spades to East's ten and your queen.
What do you reckon offers the best chance for this contract?

Example 16

Love All
Dealer West

♠ 9 5 4
♡ J 6
◇ J 7
♣ A K 6 5 4 3

| SOUTH | WEST | NORTH | EAST |
|-------|------|-------|------|
| | Pass | Pass | Pass |
| 1◇ | Pass | 2♣ | Pass |
| 2NT | Pass | 3NT | End |

♠ A 7
♡ A K 3
◇ A 9 6 5 2
♣ J 9 7

West leads the six of spades, East plays the queen and you duck. The
ten of spades appears next, won by your ace as West drops the two.
Can you find a promising line on this deal?

Example 13

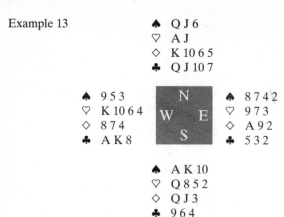

```
                    ♠  Q J 6
                    ♡  A J
                    ◇  K 10 6 5
                    ♣  Q J 10 7

   ♠  9 5 3          N          ♠  8 7 4 2
   ♡  K 10 6 4                  ♡  9 7 3
   ◇  8 7 4      W        E     ◇  A 9 2
   ♣  A K 8          S          ♣  5 3 2

                    ♠  A K 10
                    ♡  Q 8 5 2
                    ◇  Q J 3
                    ♣  9 6 4
```

As has become something of a custom, you declare 3NT. West leads the four of hearts, won by North's jack as East plays the three.

Unless East was dealt ten-nine-small in hearts, you expect to make exactly two tricks in that suit. This couple of winners, and three master spades, total to only five. You should realise that neither minor suit alone will yield the extra four tricks you need. Once you have driven out a single set of stoppers, you can score just two clubs or three diamonds. Therefore you will have to develop both suits in order to muster enough tricks.

Given that you will have to lose the lead several times, you must draw upon the positional aspect of your heart holding. Either defender can dislodge dummy's ace, but only a lead from East through the resulting ♡Q-x can profit the defence. This means that if West owns all the minor-suit tops, you are home and dry. How else might you survive?

If East has just one entry and you get rid of it first, you can whittle away West's stoppers at leisure. Of course, if East has a club honour that is not bare, the defence can arrange for West to win the first round of the suit. As that is no good, you hope East's entry lies in diamonds. Lead a diamond at trick two and pursue your attack until the ace has gone. The defence cannot counter this.

***If you need to take out one opponent's entry early, try to leave the defence with no choice about who gets in first.***

Example 14

         ♠ 9 4
         ♡ J 10 4 3
         ♢ K 8 4 2
         ♣ 8 6 2

♠ 8 6                        ♠ J 10 7 5 2
♡ 9 8 2                                          ♡ K Q 7 5
♢ A J 9 7                                        ♢ 10
♣ J 9 5 3                                        ♣ 10 7 4

         ♠ A K Q 3
         ♡ A 6
         ♢ Q 6 5 3
         ♣ A K Q

The challenge of a 3NT contract presents itself once more. West leads the three of clubs to East's ten and your king.

You have six further winners on top and can set up at least one in diamonds. Indeed, if West holds ♢A-x, you can develop three diamond tricks. After leading to the king, you would duck the next round, thereby forcing West to expend the ace on low cards. Moreover, the same play will furnish the two extra tricks you need whenever the diamonds divide 3-2. So now we dwell on the layouts in which someone has a stiff diamond.

You could elect to duck the first diamond in both hands. This might flush out a bare ace, but alas only on your left – West would surely have preferred to lead from ♢J-10-9-7 rather than a moth-eaten club suit. Perhaps you can do better than this . . .

Yes, if you lay down the queen of diamonds, you may pick up the singleton nine, ten or jack with East. Upon regaining the lead, you can then lead twice towards North's king-eight.

Finally, please note that West may switch to a middling heart after winning the ♢A. If that happens, you should play a low card from dummy and take your ace in hand. This guarantees you a double stopper in hearts however the suit lies.

***As a 4-1 break occurs fairly often, you should usually strive to cater for as many specific singletons as possible.***

Example 15

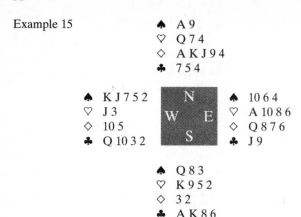

```
                    ♠  A 9
                    ♡  Q 7 4
                    ◇  A K J 9 4
                    ♣  7 5 4

    ♠  K J 7 5 2         N         ♠  10 6 4
    ♡  J 3                         ♡  A 10 8 6
    ◇  10 5        W         E     ◇  Q 8 7 6
    ♣  Q 10 3 2         S         ♣  J 9

                    ♠  Q 8 3
                    ♡  K 9 5 2
                    ◇  3 2
                    ♣  A K 8 6
```

At the wheel in 3NT you see West lead the five of spades and East beat dummy's nine with the ten. Your queen wins this.

Having four black-suit tricks, a 3-3 diamond break with the finesse right or ◇Q-10 bare onside would give you nine. Shying away from a 19% chance, you check how the hearts can help.

If you make three heart tricks, that would be fine. Sadly, you can only guarantee this if West has ♡A-J or ♡A-10 tight. On the other hand, West cannot afford to grab the ace from almost any holding of ace to three hearts. You might thus manage to score one quick heart trick before trying the diamonds. Wanting only four tricks from that suit, 4-2 with the queen right, any 3-3 split or ◇10-x with West will get you home. This sounds good, but can you do more to sway the odds in your favour?

Yes, try to sneak one heart through, but choose East as your victim. The ♡9 in your hand increases the holdings from which the defence cannot afford to rise with the ace. You simply need East to hold at least three hearts to the ace-ten or ace-jack (but not ace and two low as explained below). This represents many more chances. Besides, West might have overcalled on some hands with the ♡A. So cross to the ◇A and lead a heart.

Note that you go down if East grabs the ace from ♡A-x-x unless the ◇Q falls in two rounds. Having seen West drop the ten or the jack (from ♡J-10-x) on the second round of hearts, you may take a losing finesse into the other honour on the third.

***You may be unsure where the opposing strength lies – if so, assess which layout would benefit you the most.***

Example 16

```
              ♠ 9 5 4
              ♡ J 6
              ◇ J 7
              ♣ A K 6 5 4 3
♠ K J 8 6 2                    ♠ Q 10 3
♡ 9 8 7         N             ♡ Q 10 5 4 2
◇ 10 8 3      W   E           ◇ K Q 4
♣ Q 8           S             ♣ 10 2
              ♠ A 7
              ♡ A K 3
              ◇ A 9 6 5 2
              ♣ J 9 7
```

Having opened 1◇ in fourth seat, you and your partner enjoy a free run to 3NT. West leads the six of spades, East plays the queen and you duck. The ten of spades appears next, won by your ace as West drops the two.

If the clubs divide two apiece or the queen is bare, you can develop the suit without loss. Sadly, unless the stiff queen falls, you cannot enjoy the entire suit – your spot cards block it. Perhaps you consider conceding a club. After all, five club winners will suffice. Of course, if you lose the lead, the defence may be able to run the spades. You might give up a club to East and survive if West began with six spades. A 4-4 spade break would save you too. How do you foresee them dividing?

Since East has played back a high spade and West has petered, you tend to place at least five spades on your left. Furthermore, West's silence (no weak two or overcall of any description) inclines you to expect exactly five. Therefore you must hope the clubs play for no loser and focus on unblocking.

Cross to the ♣A at trick three. When the queen fails to drop, exit with a spade, pitching a club from hand. Upon regaining the lead, you play a second club and can claim when all follow.

***If you can predict a blockage in advance, you are better placed to do something about it.***

Example 17

Game All
Dealer South

|  | ♠ | 7 |
| ♥ | 8 6 4 2 |
| ◇ | J 7 |
| ♣ | A K 7 5 4 2 |

| SOUTH | WEST | NORTH | EAST |
|-------|------|-------|------|
| 1NT | Pass | 2♣ | Pass |
| 2♠ | Pass | 3NT | End |

♠ A K 6 5
♥ A Q
◇ K 10 5 3
♣ J 6 3

Your reply to partner's 2♣ enquiry showed four spades, but despite this West leads the ♠3. East contributes the ten and you allow it to hold. However, as a diamond shift at trick three could create a nasty guess, you win the spade jack return.

What are your further reflections on this hand?

Example 18

Game All
Dealer South

♠ Q 10 6 5
♥ K Q 9
◇ K 5
♣ J 7 5 3

| SOUTH | WEST | NORTH | EAST |
|-------|------|-------|------|
| 1NT | Pass | 2♣ | Pass |
| 2♥ | Pass | 3NT | End |

♠ A 7 2
♥ A 6 5 3
◇ A Q 7 2
♣ Q 6

West leads the club two and you play dummy's three. After a pause, East inserts the ten, which you beat with the queen.

What do you make of this first trick and of the hand overall?

Example 19

♠ Q J 5 2
♡ A K 3
♢ 10 4
♣ K Q J 8

East–West game
Dealer South

| SOUTH | WEST | NORTH | EAST |
|-------|------|--------|------|
| Pass | 1♢ | Double | Pass |
| 2♢ | Pass | 2♠ | Pass |
| 2NT | Pass | 3NT | End |

N
W    E
S

♠ A 10 4
♡ 7 6 4 2
♢ A K 5
♣ 10 9 4

West leads the queen of diamonds and East signals an odd number with the two. If, once you get in, you knock out the club ace then another high diamond will confront you.

Which do you think is the best of your various options?

Example 20

♠ 8 6 4 2
♡ A 4 3
♢ Q J 9
♣ 10 8 3

North–South game
Dealer South

| SOUTH | WEST | NORTH | EAST |
|-------|------|--------|------|
| 2♣ | Pass | 2♢ | Pass |
| 3NT | Pass | 4NT | Pass |
| 6NT | All Pass | | |

N
W    E
S

♠ A K 5
♡ K Q 8
♢ A K 10 6
♣ A K J

West tables the jack of hearts against your slam.

What is your main line of play and how might you survive even if East has spade length and the club finesse fails?

Example 17

```
             ♠ 7
             ♡ 8 6 4 2
             ◇ J 7
             ♣ A K 7 5 4 2

♠ Q 9 8 3 2      N        ♠ J 10 4
♡ J 7                     ♡ K 10 9 5 3
◇ Q 6 4     W       E     ◇ A 9 8 2
♣ Q 10 8         S        ♣ 9

             ♠ A K 6 5
             ♡ A Q
             ◇ K 10 5 3
             ♣ J 6 3
```

Even though you bid the suit en route to 3NT, West leads the ♠3, and East plays the ten. As a diamond shift at trick three could create a nasty guess, you win the spade jack return.

This time you own a double stopper in the enemy suit and no real club blockage dogs you. You might fulfil your contract with six club tricks and three outside, or with five in clubs and four elsewhere. As entries to dummy are few, it would be unwise to bash out the ace-king of clubs (dropping your jack). If the suit failed to break kindly, you could no longer make five club tricks.

Before committing yourself in clubs, you have to ascertain whether you need five tricks or six in the suit. To this end, after crossing to the club ace, you could lead either red suit. If you take a winning heart finesse, you are almost home. By contrast a diamond foray may backfire even if the suit lies well – East can just fly in with the ace. Then a heart fired through your tenace might kill you if West holds the king. A spade return may also prove fatal, as witnessed by the actual layout. You simply cannot withstand the spades being cleared while West still has a club stopper.

So take the heart finesse at trick four. When it succeeds, you can afford to give up a club next and secure your nine tricks.

***In deciding how best to acquire an extra trick, always take account of the tempo position.***

Example 18

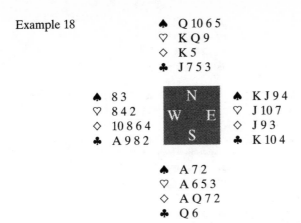

```
                    ♠ Q 10 6 5
                    ♡ K Q 9
                    ◇ K 5
                    ♣ J 7 5 3

    ♠ 8 3               N           ♠ K J 9 4
    ♡ 8 4 2        W        E       ♡ J 10 7
    ◇ 10 8 6 4                      ◇ J 9 3
    ♣ A 9 8 2           S           ♣ K 10 4

                    ♠ A 7 2
                    ♡ A 6 5 3
                    ◇ A Q 7 2
                    ♣ Q 6
```

You coast into the no-trump game via a Stayman sequence. West leads the club two and you play dummy's three. After a pause, East inserts the ten, which you beat with the queen.

For a start, East's long huddle surely confirms possession of a higher honour. You should put this knowledge to good use. Whether West has led from three clubs or four, the defenders cannot readily cash three winners in the suit. Either East's top club or West's presumed nine must block the suit.

With one club in the bag you count eight tricks. Dummy's spades offer good prospects of a ninth and a 3-3 heart division will make your fourth card in that suit good. To combine your chances, you need to avoid losing five black suit tricks (three spades plus two clubs) before you get round to testing hearts.

At trick two you should lead a *low* spade. East smothers the ten with the jack and switches to a diamond. You take this in hand and again underlead your ace of spades. Once more East captures North's honour and plays back a diamond. Dummy's king wins and now you cash your ace of spades. When one opponent shows out, you lead to the king of hearts. Paying no heed to any falsecard from East, you continue with the queen, the ace and long heart – nine tricks.

***When you have several prospective chances, try to test them in such a way as to keep all your options open.***

Example 19

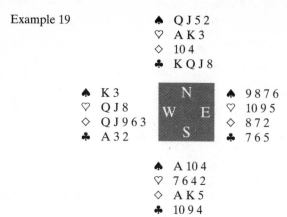

♠ Q J 5 2
♡ A K 3
◇ 10 4
♣ K Q J 8

♠ K 3
♡ Q J 8
◇ Q J 9 6 3
♣ A 3 2

♠ 9 8 7 6
♡ 10 9 5
◇ 8 7 2
♣ 7 6 5

♠ A 10 4
♡ 7 6 4 2
◇ A K 5
♣ 10 9 4

West, who opened the bidding 1◇ in second seat, leads the queen of diamonds against your 3NT contract. East signals an odd number with the two.

Knocking out the club ace will give you eight winners: three clubs, one spade and two ace-kings. If you can afford to lose the lead again, tackling spades will yield one extra. Otherwise you foresee needing a position against West.

You win trick one and lead to the king of clubs, which holds. When you continue with the queen, the ace takes it. Next West lays down the jack of diamonds, East playing the seven. An endplay looks right, or does it?

You might win now, cash North's heart tops, return to the ten of clubs and exit with a diamond. Alas, two snags spoil this little scheme. West is likely to have a third heart (and may have four clubs). Also, East ought to be able to win the diamond.

As the ♠K must be offside, your best chance is to hope that the hand on your left has a 2-3-5-3 shape. However, you do not try ducking a heart to East. Hold off the second diamond, win the third (dummy discarding a spade) and cash both remaining clubs to squeeze West. A spade pitch permits you to drop the king and a diamond discard lets you concede a spade. West's actual choice of a heart enables you to play three rounds of the suit, so setting up a long card safely.

*Running a long suit can produce an unusual benefit, such as keeping one defender off lead.*

Example 20

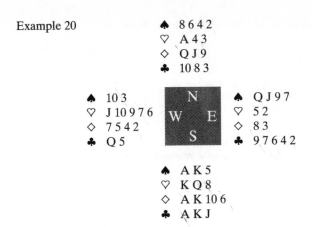

```
              ♠  8 6 4 2
              ♡  A 4 3
              ◇  Q J 9
              ♣  10 8 3

  ♠  10 3            N            ♠  Q J 9 7
  ♡  J 10 9 7 6                   ♡  5 2
  ◇  7 5 4 2      W      E        ◇  8 3
  ♣  Q 5                          ♣  9 7 6 4 2
                     S

              ♠  A K 5
              ♡  K Q 8
              ◇  A K 10 6
              ♣  A K J
```

West leads the jack of hearts against your 6NT contract.

You observe eleven winners on top and both black suits offer hope of a twelfth. Indeed, by adopting the right line, you can guarantee success if the spades split 3-3 or the queen of clubs lies where you want her.

You should picture a two-card ending in which North is on lead with one card in each black suit and you have ♣K-J. So after winning the heart, concede a spade. East likely wins and shifts to a club. You play the ♣A and next run the diamonds. Finish with your high spades, then the queen and ace of hearts.

You now have a super count on the hand. If West has saved the ♡10 or someone has run out of hearts, it will be complete.

When a spade is still out, you lead a club off dummy. If West is marked with a 4-5-3-1, you can claim as that player's other card must be a heart. In other cases you will have to decide after East follows low whether or not to finesse – anyone who had four spades and the ♣Q will have been squeezed.

You will tend to play the defender who you think (or know) began life with more clubs for the queen. On the actual hand you learn that East was dealt a 4-2-2-5 shape. So at the crucial moment, assuming East keeps a spade for the last trick, you can be certain West's ♣Q will drop. This ending, where you know to fell an honour offside, is termed a 'show-up squeeze'.

***Aim to delay a finesse or drop decision until the last moment – you may obtain a complete count on the hand.***

# 2. Declarer Play in Suit Contracts

In contested auctions both sides vie to secure their own long suit as trumps. All parties realise that the number of trumps your partnership holds correlates with the tricks you might take. Likewise many methods adopted for constructive bidding are geared towards locating the best trump suit. Even a pair of balanced hands can produce extra tricks when an eight-card fit is found, hence the widespread use of conventions such as Stayman. The constant search for the right strain reflects upon the power that trumps convey.

As declarer in a suit contract, you can employ your trump suit to serve many purposes. The long cards will score tricks in their own right and taking ruffs in the short hand frequently generates extra winners. Moreover you can stop the opponents running their long suit or perhaps ruff out dummy's side suit. Ruffing also helps you strip the hand – once you and dummy are void in the same suit, the enemy cannot lead it without conceding a ruff and discard.

Just as you must not kill a goose that lays golden eggs, you must take care not to abuse the trump suit. If you fail to draw trumps, the defenders may ruff your winners. Equally, ruffing too often can mean you run out of trumps, which may result in disaster. Thus on every hand you must judge when to play your trumps . . .

Example 21 ♠ A 8 7 4 3 2

♡ J 3

Game All ♦ A Q

Dealer South ♣ A Q 3

| SOUTH | WEST | NORTH | EAST |
|-------|------|-------|------|
| 4♡ | Pass | 4NT | Pass |
| 5♠ | Pass | 6♡ | End |

♠ 10 6 5

♡ A K Q 10 7 6 5 2

♦ 9 3

♣ —

Your 5♠ showed two key cards (two aces or, as here, one ace and the trump king) plus the trump queen. West leads the jack of clubs against your slam.

Which is the best way to try for a twelfth trick?

Example 22 ♠ 6 5 4 3

♡ —

Game All ♦ K 10 9 7 2

Dealer East ♣ 10 8 5 3

| SOUTH | WEST | NORTH | EAST |
|-------|------|-------|------|
| | | | 3♡ |
| 4♠ | 5♡ | 5♠ | Pass |
| 6♠ | All Pass | | |

♠ A K Q J 10 7

♡ A

♦ Q J 5

♣ A Q 4

Perhaps you should have doubled first and then bid 4♠, but the actual auction gave you a second chance anyway. West leads the five of hearts.

How can you make the most of your limited prospects?

Example 23

♠ 8 7 5 4
♡ J 8 4

East–West game
♦ A K 6 3

Dealer South
♣ A Q

| SOUTH | WEST | NORTH | EAST |
|-------|------|-------|------|
| 1♠ | Pass | 2♦ | Pass |
| 2♡ | Pass | 4♠ | Pass |
| 4NT | Pass | 5♡ | Pass |
| 6♠ | All Pass | | |

|   | N |   |
|---|---|---|
| W |   | E |
|   | S |   |

♠ A K 6 3 2
♡ A K Q 6
♦ J 9 4
♣ 8

Roman Key Card Blackwood crops up again, and you can work out partner's response means two aces but not the ♠Q.

West leads the five of clubs. Do you finesse?

Example 24

♠ K 10 2
♡ K J 7 3

Game All
♦ K 8 6

Dealer West
♣ 10 4 2

| SOUTH | WEST | NORTH | EAST |
|-------|------|-------|------|
|  | Pass | Pass | 1♣ |
| 1♠ | 2♣ | Double | Pass |
| 4♠ | All Pass | | |

|   | N |   |
|---|---|---|
| W |   | E |
|   | S |   |

♠ A Q 9 8 6 4 3
♡ A 9
♦ 7 5 3
♣ 5

You have agreed to play North's double as a passed hand to mean a value raise in spades. West leads the seven of clubs.

Can you find an almost foolproof line?

Example 21

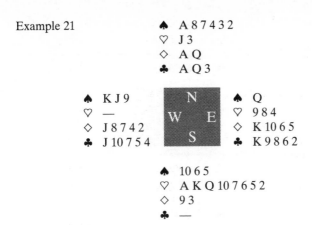

♠ A 8 7 4 3 2
♡ J 3
◇ A Q
♣ A Q 3

♠ K J 9
♡ —
◇ J 8 7 4 2
♣ J 10 7 5 4

♠ Q
♡ 9 8 4
◇ K 10 6 5
♣ K 9 8 6 2

♠ 10 6 5
♡ A K Q 10 7 6 5 2
◇ 9 3
♣ —

You have sailed in to Six Hearts. When West leads the jack of clubs, you see eleven winners comprising eight trumps and three aces. The option to finesse each minor in turn gives two bites at the cherry. However, by setting up the spades, you might improve on that.

Say you try dummy's queen at trick one and ruff East's king. You can cash the major suit aces (hearts first), throw a spade on the club ace and give up a spade. If spades fall 2-2, you are laughing unless West wins the spade and has three trumps. You also survive a 3-1 split except when West holds the length and hearts divide 3-0. Otherwise the diamond finesse always remains in reserve.

You want to cater for all the 3-1 spade and 3-0 trump breaks, but saving entries to dummy is a problem. If you duck a spade, you risk incurring a ruff, as you must do this while the ♡J sits in dummy. Going up with the ♣A does not help either. An extra entry is of no use at this stage. There must be an answer . . .

Aha! Why not throw a spade on the club king? East cannot attack dummy's diamond entry. You can win the trump shift in hand, cash the black aces (pitching a spade) and then ruff a spade. Next cross to the jack of hearts and take a second spade ruff. The spades are now good and, after you have drawn the last trump, the ◇A serves as an entry to them.

*Choosing to discard on an enemy winner can prove an effective means to keep the other defender off play.*

Example 22

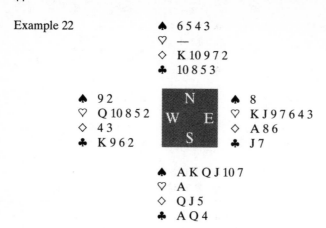

```
              ♠  6 5 4 3
              ♡  —
              ◇  K 10 9 7 2
              ♣  10 8 5 3

  ♠  9 2                      ♠  8
  ♡  Q 10 8 5 2      N        ♡  K J 9 7 6 4 3
  ◇  4 3           W   E      ◇  A 8 6
  ♣  K 9 6 2         S        ♣  J 7

              ♠  A K Q J 10 7
              ♡  A
              ◇  Q J 5
              ♣  A Q 4
```

West, who raised East's 3♡ pre-empt, leads the heart five against your contract of Six Spades. Dummy, with only one king and no trumps higher than your own seven, disappoints you somewhat. Even so, there is some sort of play for the slam.

Since you need dummy's diamonds, imagine you win East's ♡K in hand, pitching a club from table. Then you draw trumps and try to set up the diamonds. What do you think will happen?

Unless the ace of diamonds is singleton or doubleton, the defence will hold it up twice. Then you will need three tricks, and much luck, in clubs. Happily there is one glimmer of hope: the bidding suggests the ◇A and the ♣K lie in different hands. So you might be able to arrange for East to give you a ruff and discard. You will win the second diamond in dummy, take the club finesse and, assuming it works, cash the ace. Of course East will dump the king under it from an original holding of king to three. In summary you expect to handle ♣K-J doubleton, ♣K-J-x or king to four with East. In the first case the clubs play for four tricks and in the others East cannot afford to unblock.

Note the difference if you ruff the opening lead in dummy. In essence, except if trumps break 3-0 or East false-cards from ♣K-J-9-x, the above options remain alive – although you may have to endplay West instead. In addition you should be able to deal with ♣J-(x) on your right. The queen loses to the king and letting a club return run to your ace picks up the rest of the suit.

***On rare occasions plain suit cards can assume greater value than trumps – bear this in mind.***

Example 23

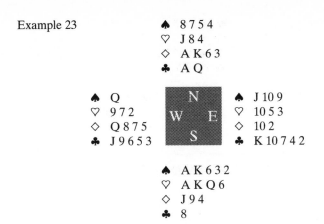

```
              ♠  8 7 5 4
              ♡  J 8 4
              ◇  A K 6 3
              ♣  A Q

    ♠  Q              N           ♠  J 10 9
    ♡  9 7 2                      ♡  10 5 3
    ◇  Q 8 7 5    W       E       ◇  10 2
    ♣  J 9 6 5 3      S           ♣  K 10 7 4 2

              ♠  A K 6 3 2
              ♡  A K Q 6
              ◇  J 9 4
              ♣  8
```

West leads the five of clubs against your 6♠, giving you a crucial guess at trick one. You must plan how to resolve it.

You expected a club lead since your side bid the other three suits. Given the lack of values in the East-West hands and the state of the score, their silence says nothing either.

West could have led from the ten, the jack or small cards. The five may also be from a suit headed by the king, king-ten or king-jack. The club finesse is almost a 50-50 shot (in fact West has the king in 77 of the 156 possible club holdings). Where does this leave you?

You can assume a 3-1 trump break or your play will hardly matter. So if you decline the club finesse, you will try to endplay the defender with the third trump. The basic line for this is: win with the ♣A, draw two trumps and cross to the ◇A. Then ruff a club, cash your hearts and play a spade.

That way you succeed if the defender with three trumps has the ◇Q as you can put up your jack or run the lead round to it (45%). The same line wins if this opponent holds one diamond (5%) – you get a ruff and discard. In addition, when East is your victim, you pick up the doubleton ten (2%) – East has to exit with the ten, which you cover. Moreover, if someone shows up with three trumps and four (or five) hearts, you can play that person for two diamonds. You then cash a second diamond before exiting. This boosts your chance of success when one defender has a singleton trump above the basic total of 52%.

***In comparing two distinct lines ensure you include all the winning chances in your reckoning.***

Example 24

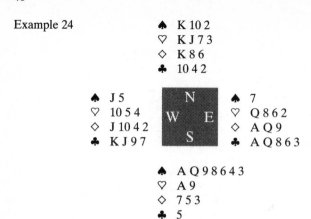

```
                    ♠ K 10 2
                    ♡ K J 7 3
                    ◇ K 8 6
                    ♣ 10 4 2

   ♠ J 5              N            ♠ 7
   ♡ 10 5 4                        ♡ Q 8 6 2
   ◇ J 10 4 2     W      E         ◇ A Q 9
   ♣ K J 9 7         S             ♣ A Q 8 6 3

                    ♠ A Q 9 8 6 4 3
                    ♡ A 9
                    ◇ 7 5 3
                    ♣ 5
```

You have come back down to earth with game in spades. West leads the seven of clubs and you survey dummy's flat but well-fitting hand. You want to find as safe a line as possible.

You can spot nine easy tricks by way of seven spades and two hearts. Somehow you will need to utilise dummy's red suit holdings to build a tenth. After drawing trumps you can cash the ace of hearts and take the heart finesse. If that fails, you will remain in the hunt because you can lead towards the ◇K later. As you can see, both key honours are offside. So down you go.

On the bidding you place the ace of diamonds on your right and the best play even with no clue is to throw East in. You intend to trump the second club, cross to the king of spades and ruff dummy's last club. Afterwards you will cash the major suit aces and lead the nine of hearts, planning to run it. If West produces the ten, you will play North's jack, which will stump East just the same. Apart from East having three trumps, what might go wrong?

Well, if you forget to call for the ten of clubs at trick one, a smart opponent may allow West's seven to hold! A shift to the ◇J would then beat you for sure. By forcing East to win now, you keep West off play and ensure that the return will help you strip the hand.

***If you fall asleep at trick one then there may be no point waking up later.***

Example 25

♠ J
♡ A 6 2
♦ K Q 9 8 7 5 2
♣ Q 9

Game All
Dealer South

| SOUTH | WEST | NORTH | EAST |
|-------|------|-------|------|
| 1♦ | Pass | 2♦ | Pass |
| 2NT | Pass | 4NT | Pass |
| 5♣ | Pass | 5NT | Pass |
| 6♡ | Pass | 7♦ | End |

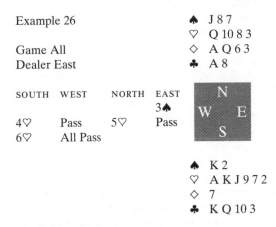

♠ A K 5
♡ K 9 5
♦ A J 6 4
♣ A 5 4

Your side's two-level bids were both forcing. Later you showed three aces and two kings. No doubt partner was hoping one of the latter would be in clubs, in which case the ♣Q would be the thirteenth trick.

Plan the play on the ♣J lead, taking all the time you need.

Example 26

♠ J 8 7
♡ Q 10 8 3
♦ A Q 6 3
♣ A 8

Game All
Dealer East

| SOUTH | WEST | NORTH | EAST |
|-------|------|-------|------|
|  |  |  | 3♠ |
| 4♡ | Pass | 5♡ | Pass |
| 6♡ | All Pass |  |  |

♠ K 2
♡ A K J 9 7 2
♦ 7
♣ K Q 10 3

West leads the three of spades and you rightly stop to think before playing from dummy.

Are alarm bells ringing, if so, how might you silence them?

Example 25

```
              ♠  J
              ♡  A 6 2
              ◇  K Q 9 8 7 5 2
              ♣  Q 9

♠ Q 10 8 7 3          N          ♠  9 6 4 2
♡ Q 10 8 4      W         E      ♡  J 7 3
◇ 10                S           ◇  3
♣ J 10 8                        ♣  K 7 6 3 2

              ♠  A K 5
              ♡  K 9 5
              ◇  A J 6 4
              ♣  A 5 4
```

Whilst heading the field in a National event, the Pachabo cup for the English inter-county teams of four, you find yourself in 7◇. West leads the jack of clubs and you realise you have work to do.

The spade suit offers a Chinese finesse – you can run the jack of spades, hoping East has the queen but omits to cover. Surely more appealing prospects than this must exist.

If either defender has sole control of hearts (at least five cards or the ♡Q-J-10), a simple squeeze between the rounded suits ought to work. If instead someone holds seven spades (or ♠Q-10-9-8-7-6) a black suit squeeze should be on. That is less likely, but you can defer a full decision on which to play for until later. In either case you would have to judge who to leave in charge of clubs. Ducking in dummy at trick one retains a threat against East's presumed king. Covering with the queen will transfer control to West. Which should you do?

By compelling West to look after the clubs, you greatly enhance the contract's chances. Even if it is your right-hand opponent guarding a major, you will still set up a squeeze – but a double squeeze instead of a single one. Indeed, provided you read the ending correctly, you need no longer care how the major suits divide. Simply rattle off seven rounds of diamonds, pitching two clubs and a heart from hand.

Let us examine the expected end position with two rounds of trumps still to go:

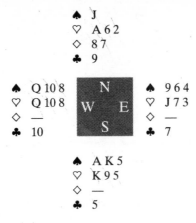

```
                    ♠  J
                    ♡  A 6 2
                    ◇  8 7
                    ♣  9

    ♠  Q 10 8          N          ♠  9 6 4
    ♡  Q 10 8     W        E      ♡  J 7 3
    ◇  —                          ◇  —
    ♣  10             S           ♣  7

                    ♠  A K 5
                    ♡  K 9 5
                    ◇  —
                    ♣  5
```

West has two tricky discards to find and will probably come down to three cards in one major and a singleton in the other, together with the ten of clubs of course. East can spare the seven of clubs but, equally reduced to five cards, will have to abandon the major West has kept. In the meantime you can safely part with your last club and a low heart.

To finish West off, you need to cash the king and ace of the suit that you judge East to have saved. However, it is safe to take the ♡K when the hand on your left has kept spades, and doing so may make the position clearer. Therefore you should do that first. Assuming West hangs on to the ten of clubs to the bitter end, either the ♡6 or the ♠5 will score.

Note that a compound squeeze nearly always involves an element of guesswork. Here the fact that you could run all of your long suit before deciding how who was keeping what improved your likelihood of success. Having started off with fairly equal lengths in the majors, West had little real chance of deceiving you.

You could have used the ♡9 as the heart threat, but then you would have been more likely to get the ending wrong. You would have had to decide what was going on after seeing only one forced discard from West.

*A threat placed over a stopper is worth much more than a menace sitting under a guard.*

Example 26

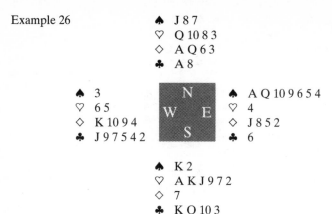

&spades; J 8 7
&hearts; Q 10 8 3
&diams; A Q 6 3
&clubs; A 8

&spades; 3
&hearts; 6 5
&diams; K 10 9 4
&clubs; J 9 7 5 4 2

&spades; A Q 10 9 6 5 4
&hearts; 4
&diams; J 8 5 2
&clubs; 6

&spades; K 2
&hearts; A K J 9 7 2
&diams; 7
&clubs; K Q 10 3

You brush aside East's 3&spades; opening and climb up to a small slam in hearts. West leads the three of spades and you must form a plan.

With the lead coming up to your king of spades, it may seem you simply need to draw trumps and ruff the fourth club in dummy. Sadly a major snag threatens to scotch this plan.

East's pre-emptive spade bid and West's three tell you the lead is a singleton. Unless you drop the king under the ace at trick one, a spade return ruffed will kill you stone dead. So, for a start, you must part with your king of spades in the same calm manner you would use if you had no choice about it.

We now suppose that East falls for this ruse and shifts to a passive heart. After drawing trumps, two principal ways to deal with your losing spade present themselves. You can arrange to ruff two diamonds in hand, keeping the club finesse in reserve if the diamond king is still out. Instead you can try to drop the jack of clubs, with the diamond finesse as your fall back.

On two counts the latter line is better: the spade length on your right makes West favourite to hold any unseen minor-suit honour; also a picture will come down in three rounds more often from seven cards than from eight.

***When you know you will go down on normal play, look to fool the enemy about your hand and do so smoothly.***

Example 27

East–West game
Dealer East

♠ 7 5 4 3 2
♡ A
◇ K Q J
♣ K Q 6 4

| SOUTH | WEST | NORTH | EAST |
|-------|------|-------|------|
|       |      |       | 1♠   |
| 2◇    | Pass | 2♠    | Pass |
| 3◇    | Pass | 3♠    | Pass |
| 4♡    | Pass | 5◇    | End  |

♠ 9 6
♡ Q 9 8 4
◇ A 9 8 6 4 2
♣ A

North's first cue-bid showed a value raise and the second asked for further description.

East overtakes West's ♠J lead and plays two more spades, West throwing a club at the second trick.

If trumps do not break quite as you would like, how can you nonetheless collect the rest of the tricks?

Example 28

Game All
Dealer West

♠ A J 6 2
♡ K 9 4 2
◇ 10 7
♣ Q 10 4

| SOUTH   | WEST     | NORTH | EAST |
|---------|----------|-------|------|
|         | Pass     | Pass  | 3♣   |
| Double  | Pass     | 4♣    | Pass |
| 4♡      | All Pass |       |      |

♠ Q 7 4 3
♡ A J 10 6
◇ K Q J
♣ K 8

West cheerily leads the six of clubs to East's ace. West ruffs the club two return and switches to the diamond three. East produces another ace and shoots back a further club.

What are your plans for playing both majors without loss?

Example 27

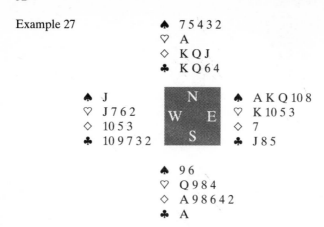

```
                    ♠ 7 5 4 3 2
                    ♡ A
                    ◇ K Q J
                    ♣ K Q 6 4

   ♠ J              ┌─────────┐       ♠ A K Q 10 8
   ♡ J 7 6 2        │    N    │       ♡ K 10 5 3
   ◇ 10 5 3         │  W   E  │       ◇ 7
   ♣ 10 9 7 3 2     │    S    │       ♣ J 8 5
                    └─────────┘
                    ♠ 9 6
                    ♡ Q 9 8 4
                    ◇ A 9 8 6 4 2
                    ♣ A
```

You play in Five Diamonds after East has opened One Spade. East overtakes West's ♠J and plays two more spades, West throwing a club at trick two.

You will want to start by ruffing high – the spade layout means that West rates to hold the ten of diamonds. Besides, if trumps split 2-2 or the ten is a singleton, you can still manage to draw them and trump a heart loser in dummy.

After ruffing in with the ace, you lead a diamond, but the ten does not appear. Might you yet survive a 3-1 trump break?

You believe you have threats against East in each major, but entries are a problem. You must go for a trump squeeze (i.e., one in which you ruff something after the squeeze has taken place). This will allow access to the ♡Q if need be. Moreover, as the ♡A is North's sole late entry, dummy needs to win the squeeze trick. Assuming you decide to draw trumps first, this will come about on North's second club winner.

As the squeeze card will be a plain-suit winner, East will feel pressure only when you are down to one trump (a standard feature of trump squeezes). Now at this stage you have two more diamonds than dummy. Therefore, you need to ruff a club in hand before drawing trumps. Unblock the ♣A at trick five and then play a second diamond. When East shows out, you trump a club, pull the last trump and play dummy's king-queen of clubs. This end position results:

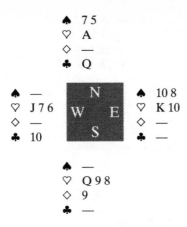

```
            ♠  7 5
            ♥  A
            ♦  —
            ♣  Q

    ♠  —              ♠  10 8
    ♥  J 7 6          ♥  K 10
    ♦  —             ♦  —
    ♣  10            ♣  —

            ♠  —
            ♥  Q 9 8
            ♦  9
            ♣  —
```

If on the club queen East pitches a spade, you ruff the suit good and the ace of hearts gives an entry to the winning spade. If instead East discards a heart, the ace drops the king, leaving your hand high.

Note that although ruffing one club made no difference to your tally of trump tricks, it proved an essential move on this deal. Dummy reversals can be difficult to spot at the best of times – all the more so when they involve but a single ruff and yield only an indirect benefit. You would doubtless feel pleased if you got this hand right at the table.

If you will forgive a diversion, suppose now that East passed as dealer and the first four tricks went the same way. In this case you place West with the king of hearts and must hope for a criss-cross squeeze. One of those can work if West was dealt ♥K-J-10-(x) and any five or more clubs. You avoid touching the rounded suits early, taking three rounds of trumps and ruffing a spade to hand. When you table your final trump West is likely to be looking at king and another heart as well as four clubs. If this defender discards a club, you must throw dummy's last spade and cash the club ace to leave dummy high. West may prefer to shed a heart since that could save the day if East held the ♥9 or the ♥8. Then you cross to the ♥A, come back to the ♣A and make the remaining three tricks with your ♥Q-9-8.

*Trumps can really come to the rescue when you lack the entries for the more usual types of squeeze.*

54

Example 28

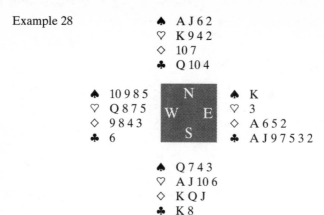

```
                              ♠ A J 6 2
                              ♡ K 9 4 2
                              ◇ 10 7
                              ♣ Q 10 4

        ♠ 10 9 8 5          N              ♠ K
        ♡ Q 8 7 5       W       E          ♡ 3
        ◇ 9 8 4 3                          ◇ A 6 5 2
        ♣ 6                 S              ♣ A J 9 7 5 3 2

                              ♠ Q 7 4 3
                              ♡ A J 10 6
                              ◇ K Q J
                              ♣ K 8
```

East pre-empts Three Clubs in third seat and you reach 4♡. West gaily leads the six of clubs to East's ace. West ruffs the club two return and shifts to the three of diamonds. East turns up with an ace here too and fires back a further club.

You must start by deciding whether to ruff high or not. This is easy enough. With seven clubs and the ace of diamonds dealt to East, much more space exists on your left for the queen of hearts. In addition, since you must avoid losing a spade, you may require East to have three low in that suit (giving West a doubleton king). Finally, as East would no doubt have cashed the ace of diamonds at trick two if it were bare, you can place at least two diamonds on your right. Therefore, you ruff in with your ace and finesse West for the queen of hearts. After drawing three rounds of those (remember West ruffed once), do you still need to do something special?

You can lead a spade to the jack, but is that likely to help? You already think you know ten of East's cards: seven clubs, two diamonds and a heart. If you cash your winning diamonds and East follows to both, West cannot hold ♠K-x. Starting with the queen and having it covered is no better. Having got to this point only one hope remains: lead to dummy's ace and pray that you fell the stiff king.

*Avoid a futile line by counting the total cards held by your opponents.*

Example 29

Game All
Dealer East

♠ K
♡ K J 10 3
◇ A J 8 7
♣ Q 6 3 2

| SOUTH | WEST | NORTH | EAST |
|-------|------|-------|------|
|       |      |       | 1♣   |
| 3♠    | Pass | 4♠    | End  |

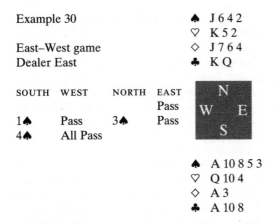

♠ A J 10 9 8 6 3
♡ Q 9 6
◇ 10 6 4
♣ —

West faithfully leads the jack of clubs, which you ruff in hand as East plays the four.

How should you proceed?

Example 30

East–West game
Dealer East

♠ J 6 4 2
♡ K 5 2
◇ J 7 6 4
♣ K Q

| SOUTH | WEST | NORTH | EAST |
|-------|------|-------|------|
|       |      |       | Pass |
| 1♠    | Pass | 3♠    | Pass |
| 4♠    | All Pass |    |      |

♠ A 10 8 5 3
♡ Q 10 4
◇ A 3
♣ A 10 8

West starts with the four of clubs, which is won by the queen whilst East plays the two.

How will you tackle the trumps and what will you do if their lie is okay but less than ideal?

Example 29

```
              ♠  K
              ♡  K J 10 3
              ◇  A J 8 7
              ♣  Q 6 3 2

  ♠ Q 7 4 2        N          ♠  5
  ♡ 8 5                        ♡  A 7 4 2
  ◇ K 3 2      W       E       ◇  Q 9 5
  ♣ J 10 8 7       S           ♣  A K 9 5 4

              ♠  A J 10 9 8 6 3
              ♡  Q 9 6
              ◇  10 6 4
              ♣  —
```

West leads the jack of East's bid club suit against your spade game. You ruff in hand as East plays the four.

The enemy's ♡A must score and you expect to lose a trump as well. You may also have two diamond losers, but dummy's hearts should provide a haven for one of them. The defence cannot dislodge North's ace of diamonds entry without giving you two tricks in the suit. So what might upset the apple cart?

Suppose you lead a low spade to dummy's king, ruff a club to hand, and play ace and another trump. Whoever wins with the queen can continue clubs, making you ruff a third time (or West plays a diamond first if out of clubs). If trumps break 4-1, you will then be in trouble. Drawing them will allow the defence to cash a club or two when you knock out the ♡A; not drawing them means you may incur a ruff. The slender chance of West having a club shortage and key cards in the red suits might save you, but not today.

You fare no better if you return to hand at trick three with the queen of hearts. Once West obtains the lead, a heart across to East's ace and a heart back will allow West to ruff.

To overcome these hazards, you should lay down the ace of spades at trick two, crashing North's king. You can then safely drive out the defender's queen of spades and retain control. This line only backfires if someone has queen to three trumps coupled with a small singleton heart.

*Take care to preserve your trump length – even with a seven-card suit you can lose control.*

Example 30

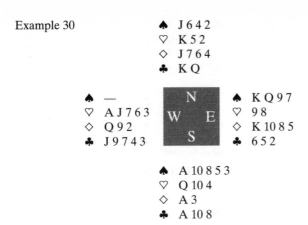

```
              ♠  J 6 4 2
              ♡  K 5 2
              ◇  J 7 6 4
              ♣  K Q

  ♠  —                        ♠  K Q 9 7
  ♡  A J 7 6 3                ♡  9 8
  ◇  Q 9 2                    ◇  K 10 8 5
  ♣  J 9 7 4 3                ♣  6 5 2

              ♠  A 10 8 5 3
              ♡  Q 10 4
              ◇  A 3
              ♣  A 10 8
```

Again you declare 4♠. West starts with the four of clubs, which is won by the queen whilst East plays the two.

As dummy contains just five cards in the rounded suits, you predict only one heart loser. After drawing trumps you intend to throw a heart from dummy on the third club. So success mainly hinges on limiting the defence to one trump winner. Ruling out ♠K-Q-x-(x) offside, we consider how you might do this.

Leading low to the ten costs whenever you find a stiff honour or a void on your left. Playing to the ace backfires when West holds either a void or a singleton seven or nine. Running the jack goes wrong if East covers with a bare honour or West has king-queen tight (you finesse next time or a singleton honour offside beats you). To sum up, all the above plays have three ways to lose. By contrast, finessing the eight ought to work well unless West's spades are a lone nine or king-queen doubleton – just two losing layouts. True, life may become tricky on a 4-0 break, but you can handle that, making it only a minor factor.

Once West discards on your eight, you should lead to the king of hearts. Then unblock the king of clubs and lead a trump, forcing East to split honours. After making the ace of spades, you throw a heart on a club, exit with the ♡Q, and later ruff the third heart high.

*When you have a number of options, go for the one with the fewest losing cases.*

58

Example 31

East–West game
Dealer North

|  | ♠ | A K J |
| --- | --- | --- |
|  | ♡ | Q 9 6 4 |
|  | ◊ | A K 7 3 |
|  | ♣ | A 5 |

| SOUTH | WEST | NORTH | EAST |
| --- | --- | --- | --- |
|  |  | 2NT | Pass |
| 3◊ | Pass | 3♠ | Pass |
| 4♡ | All Pass |  |  |

♠ Q 6 3
♡ J 8 7 5 3
◊ Q 10 6 2
♣ 7

Partner's 3♠ break means you wind up as declarer in spite of using a transfer. West starts off with the four of clubs, which is captured by North's ace. East follows with the two, showing an odd number.

What is the best way to broach the trumps?

Example 32

East–West game
Dealer East

|  | ♠ | 5 2 |
| --- | --- | --- |
|  | ♡ | A 9 4 |
|  | ◊ | Q 10 5 |
|  | ♣ | A Q 10 8 4 |

| SOUTH | WEST | NORTH | EAST |
| --- | --- | --- | --- |
|  |  |  | Pass |
| 1♠ | Pass | 2♣ | Pass |
| 2♡ | Pass | 3◊ | Pass |
| 3♡ | Pass | 4♡ | End |

♠ Q 8 7 6 4
♡ Q J 10 8 5
◊ —
♣ K J 9

An aggressive opening bid propels you into game, against which West leads the two of hearts. East wins the first trick with the trump king and returns the suit, all following.

Nine tricks are easy to find; from where will you get a tenth?

Example 33

Love All
Dealer East

♠ A K Q J 9 2
♡ 8 5 2
◇ 6
♣ J 9 4

| SOUTH | WEST | NORTH | EAST |
|-------|------|-------|------|
|       |      |       | Pass |
| 1NT   | Pass | 2♡    | Pass |
| 2♠    | Pass | 4♠    | End  |

```
        N
    W       E
        S
```

♠ 6 4
♡ Q J 4
◇ A Q J 7
♣ K 7 5 2

A weak no-trump and simple transfer put you in the spade game. West starts off with club eight. This is covered by the nine, ten and king.

How do you hope to land this contract?

Example 34

Game All
Dealer North

♠ 9 5 4 2
♡ A J 3
◇ A Q
♣ Q J 7 2

| SOUTH | WEST | NORTH | EAST |
|-------|------|-------|------|
|       |      | 1♣    | 1♡   |
| 1♠    | 3♡   | 3♠    | 4♡   |
| 4♠    | Pass | Pass  | Double |
| All Pass |   |       |      |

```
        N
    W       E
        S
```

♠ Q J 8 7 6 3
♡ 10
◇ K J 10 7 2
♣ 3

West, who seems unhappy about the final double, leads the four of hearts.

How do you prove that your opponent's concern is justified?

Example 31

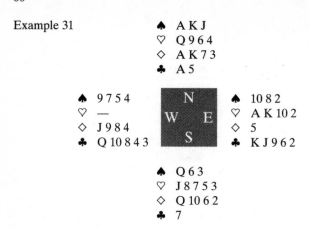

♠ A K J
♡ Q 9 6 4
◇ A K 7 3
♣ A 5

♠ 9 7 5 4
♡ —
◇ J 9 8 4
♣ Q 10 8 4 3

♠ 10 8 2
♡ A K 10 2
◇ 5
♣ K J 9 6 2

♠ Q 6 3
♡ J 8 7 5 3
◇ Q 10 6 2
♣ 7

Your contract is Four Hearts and West starts off with the four of clubs, which North's ace duly despatches. East follows with the two, denoting an odd number.

Your contract looks a pushover. Most of the time you would forecast an overtrick, simply losing two trumps. Of course, the very fact that it appears here will inspire you to look closer!

A 4-0 trump break might make things awkward, but you have no real clue about which defender has trump length. North's 2NT opening will have deterred East-West from coming in, red against green, pretty well whatever their shape. Moreover you read the missing clubs as splitting 5-5. What do you have to go on?

You can afford to concede three heart tricks provided the diamond suit runs without hiccup. Knowing only ◇J-x-x-x-(x) on your left will create a diamond loser, you should presume such a position exists. Once you infer that one opponent holds long diamonds, the other becomes favourite to have four trumps. So you tackle the hearts by advancing dummy's queen. East wins and leads a club, forcing you to ruff. Staying with the theory that West has diamond length, you use a couple of dummy's entries in spades to lead through East twice more. You thereby restrict your trump losses to two.

*If only one lie of the cards will trouble you, assume such a layout exists and place the other cards to fit in with it.*

Example 32

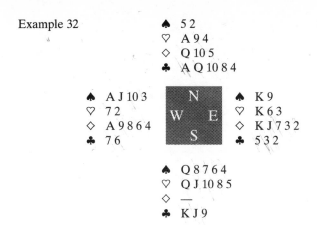

```
              ♠  5 2
              ♡  A 9 4
              ◇  Q 10 5
              ♣  A Q 10 8 4

♠  A J 10 3          ♠  K 9
♡  7 2              ♡  K 6 3
◇  A 9 8 6 4        ◇  K J 7 3 2
♣  7 6              ♣  5 3 2

              ♠  Q 8 7 6 4
              ♡  Q J 10 8 5
              ◇  —
              ♣  K J 9
```

You reach the heart game and West leads the two of hearts, which you decide to duck in dummy. East wins the first trick with the trump king and returns the suit, all following.

Having nine obvious winners, you no doubt wonder whether the queen of spades could also score. What clues are on offer?

Well, as West did not lead the ace of diamonds, you place a top honour in that suit on your right. So East, who passed as dealer and has already produced the king of hearts, cannot have the ace-king in spades. Besides, West's choice of a trump attack hints at strong spades on your left. If spades will not yield a trick, maybe you can ruff one instead . . .

If East holds ♠J-(3), ♠10-(3) or ♠9-(3) then you can duck spades to West, who you assume does not hold the remaining trump – many people lead the middle one from three trumps, meaning the two implies a doubleton. So that way you might set up a third-round spade ruff. The avoidance play enhances your prospects, but can you better this?

Yes indeed, a dummy reversal will work if the defender with the third trump also has three or four clubs. Use a heart now, the club ten and the club queen as entries to ruff diamonds in hand. Then cross to the ace of clubs, pull the outstanding trump and claim.

*Taking a series of ruffs in the original long trump hand and drawing trumps with the other can gain you a trick.*

Example 33

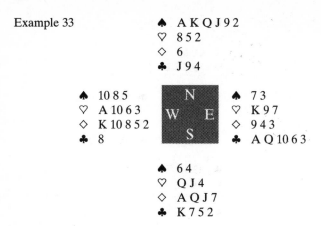

```
              ♠  A K Q J 9 2
              ♡  8 5 2
              ◇  6
              ♣  J 9 4

   ♠  10 8 5         N          ♠  7 3
   ♡  A 10 6 3                  ♡  K 9 7
   ◇  K 10 8 5 2  W       E     ◇  9 4 3
   ♣  8               S         ♣  A Q 10 6 3

              ♠  6 4
              ♡  Q J 4
              ◇  A Q J 7
              ♣  K 7 5 2
```

Although 3NT looks a tad easier, you are back in spades, but still at the four level. West starts off with the eight of clubs. When that card is covered by the nine, ten and king in turn, you assess how to proceed.

You aim to draw trumps and at some point lead hearts twice towards your hand. You expect to develop a heart trick since West, who did not lead the suit at trick one, can hardly have ♡A-K. Of course, this play fails to address a more pressing matter. Now your club stopper has gone, the defenders will be able to cash two clubs and two hearts if they obtain the lead. To counter that threat you must get rid of one of your clubs on a winning diamond.

You can cross to dummy with a trump to take the diamond finesse, but do you really believe it will succeed? The opening lead marks the ace-queen of clubs on your right and we have worked out that a heart honour lies there too. So, knowing East would not pass in first seat with twelve points, you can place the king of diamonds with West. Alas, you lack the entries to take a ruffing finesse and come back quickly to your hand . . .

Rather than give up, you should table the jack of diamonds at trick two! Keen to see East win and lead a club back, West may well duck this. If the jack holds, you smartly cash the ace of diamonds, disposing of a small club from dummy.

***Only when normal play seems destined to fail should you rely on a defensive misjudgement.***

Example 34

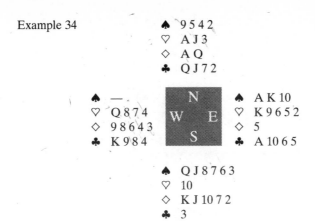

♠ 9 5 4 2
♡ A J 3
◇ A Q
♣ Q J 7 2

♠ —
♡ Q 8 7 4
◇ 9 8 6 4 3
♣ K 9 8 4

♠ A K 10
♡ K 9 6 5 2
◇ 5
♣ A 10 6 5

♠ Q J 8 7 6 3
♡ 10
◇ K J 10 7 2
♣ 3

After the opposing side has competed to Four Hearts, you declare Four Spades Doubled. West leads the four of hearts.

You place the doubler with three trumps, but this is not in itself a problem. Perhaps you simply put up North's heart ace at trick one and then try a trump. East flies in with a big trump and switches coolly to the five of diamonds. Still not seeing the danger, some would play a second spade. East jumps on this, underleads the ace of clubs, and the ensuing diamond ruff sinks your contract.

Maybe, once East decided to grab the first trump and play back a diamond, you foresaw the impending ruff. In an attempt to cut West off you might then lead the jack of hearts at trick four. You plan to discard a club on it if East hastily covers with the king, or otherwise hope that this same opponent holds the ace-king of clubs. Sadly, against competent defence, neither wish comes true.

Before touching trumps you must break the link between the defenders. Return a heart at trick two, pitching your stiff club, or just concede a club. Either way West is out of the picture. You ruff any return and the ace of diamonds vitally lets dummy lead trumps once.

*To avert an adverse ruff you should try to attack the defenders' entries before they play their short suit.*

Example 35

&spades; A 6 4
&hearts; 7 5 4

Game All
Dealer South

&diams; J 7
&clubs; A Q 8 3 2

| SOUTH | WEST | NORTH | EAST |
|-------|------|-------|------|
| 1&hearts; | Pass | 2&clubs; | Pass |
| 2&hearts; | Pass | 3&hearts; | Pass |
| 4&hearts; | All Pass | | |

&spades; 10 5 2
&hearts; A K J 10 3
&diams; Q 10
&clubs; K J 5

When your partner's hand comes down you reckon the two-suit fit compensates for the doubleton diamond in each hand. West leads the queen of spades, East following.

How do you plan the play?

Example 36

&spades; 10 5
&hearts; J 7 6 3

East–West game
Dealer South

&diams; A J 10 7 6
&clubs; A 10

| SOUTH | WEST | NORTH | EAST |
|-------|------|-------|------|
| 1&hearts; | 2&hearts;* | 4&diams; | Pass |
| 4&hearts; | 4&spades; | Pass | Pass |
| 5&hearts; | All Pass | | |

* spades and a minor

&spades; K 6
&hearts; A K Q 10 9 4
&diams; 9 8 5 2
&clubs; 6

West's 2&hearts; cue bid showed spades and another suit. The opening lead is the king of clubs, which you win in dummy.

How you propose to score ten more tricks?

Example 37

North–South game
Dealer North

|  | | ♠ | K 10 7 6 5 2 |
|---|---|---|---|
|  | | ♡ | A J 10 |
|  | | ◇ | Q 9 |
|  | | ♣ | J 2 |

| SOUTH | WEST | NORTH | EAST |
|-------|------|-------|------|
|       |      | 1♠    | Pass |
| 2♡    | Pass | 3♡    | Pass |
| 4NT   | Pass | 5◇    | Pass |
| 6♡    | All Pass |    |      |

|  | | ♠ | A |
|---|---|---|---|
|  | | ♡ | K 8 7 6 5 4 |
|  | | ◇ | A K |
|  | | ♣ | K 9 8 3 |

West leads the diamond six and a slightly misfitting dummy means you may have an uphill struggle. If North's queen were in any of the other suits, your chances would be better.

What do you reckon is your best hope on the actual deal?

Example 38

Game All
Dealer South

|  | | ♠ | K 9 6 5 |
|---|---|---|---|
|  | | ♡ | A J 9 8 3 |
|  | | ◇ | 7 6 |
|  | | ♣ | Q 9 |

| SOUTH | WEST | NORTH | EAST |
|-------|------|-------|------|
| 1NT   | Pass | 2◇    | Pass |
| 3♡    | Pass | 4♡    | End  |

|  | | ♠ | A 7 3 |
|---|---|---|---|
|  | | ♡ | K Q 7 6 |
|  | | ◇ | Q J |
|  | | ♣ | A J 6 2 |

With the queen-jack of diamonds of doubtful value, your decision to break the transfer was a marginal one. As it turns out partner was always going to put you in game.

West starts off with the eight of spades.

What is your strategy to avoid four losers?

Example 35

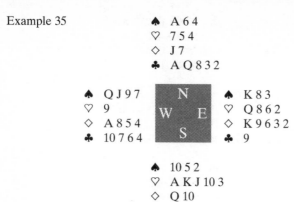

♠ A 6 4
♡ 7 5 4
◇ J 7
♣ A Q 8 3 2

♠ Q J 9 7          ♠ K 8 3
♡ 9                ♡ Q 8 6 2
◇ A 8 5 4          ◇ K 9 6 3 2
♣ 10 7 6 4         ♣ 9

♠ 10 5 2
♡ A K J 10 3
◇ Q 10
♣ K J 5

After a simple sequence you arrive in Four Hearts. West leads the queen of spades, East following.

You locate two losers in spades, two in diamonds, and a hole in trumps as well. Although a 5-2 spade division might deny the defence one of their spade winners (if East holds both top diamonds and West wins a trump), a second undertrick is a minor matter. For the main objective, making your contract, you must aim to run at least ten tricks without giving up the lead.

You can ill afford to try a top trump before taking the finesse. When East has ♡Q-x-x-x you would have to overtake two clubs to reach dummy twice more and need ♣10-9 to be stiff. Even if hearts were 3-2, most 4-1 club breaks would also defeat you – in addition to picking up the trumps you need four club tricks.

The best play, having put up the ace of spades, is to finesse the jack of trumps at trick two. Once this holds, you follow with the ace, getting bad news when West's diamond eight appears. You should now play the king of clubs to dummy's ace, noting the fall of the nine on your right. After that you can repeat the heart finesse, extract the defender's last trump and lead the jack of clubs. East shows out on this second club. Now, thanks to your foresight in overtaking on the first round, you reach a marked finesse position and can run the rest of the suit.

**When you have to play suits in an abnormal way, think about the wider effects of doing so.**

Example 36

♠ 10 5
♡ J 7 6 3
◇ A J 10 7 6
♣ A 10

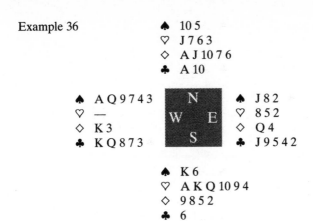

♠ A Q 9 7 4 3
♡ —
◇ K 3
♣ K Q 8 7 3

♠ J 8 2
♡ 8 5 2
◇ Q 4
♣ J 9 5 4 2

♠ K 6
♡ A K Q 10 9 4
◇ 9 8 5 2
♣ 6

You have been pushed to Five Hearts by West, who has shown a big two-suiter with preference for spades. Dummy's ace takes the king of clubs opening lead.

With no bidding to guide you, the normal line is to draw trumps and finesse the diamonds. That succeeds either if West has at least one diamond honour and East the spade ace or if West holds all three key honours. The actual sequence marks the opponent on your left with a strong hand, almost certainly including six spades and five clubs . . .

West surely possesses the ace of spades but scarcely has room for the king-queen of diamonds. Given that standard play will likely mean defeat, you must try something else. You will have to aim to develop the diamonds without letting East in.

Provided West's diamonds consist of the king and any other card, you could be in luck. You need to attack diamonds from hand, planning to play dummy's ace on the opposite trick to the king. Can anything foil this specific avoidance strategy?

Having reasoned that West was dealt eleven black cards and two diamonds, you can read the trumps as being 0-3. If you try to come over with a trump, this defender might work out to jettison the king of diamonds. So use a club ruff at trick two to get to hand and then play on diamonds.

***Once you have formed a good plan, do not give the defence even half of a chance to spoil it.***

Example 37

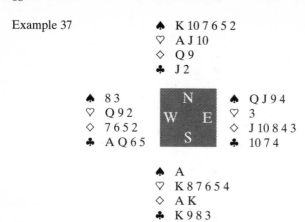

♠ K 10 7 6 5 2
♡ A J 10
♢ Q 9
♣ J 2

♠ 8 3               ♠ Q J 9 4
♡ Q 9 2            ♡ 3
♢ 7 6 5 2          ♢ J 10 8 4 3
♣ A Q 6 5         ♣ 10 7 4

♠ A
♡ K 8 7 6 5 4
♢ A K
♣ K 9 8 3

With no clues from the bidding to help, you have to make twelve tricks with hearts as trumps. West leads the ♢6.

You face a possible trump loser and the club position is somewhat tenuous. After unblocking the ace of spades you can cash the king and ace of hearts, hoping the queen falls. If it does, you take the king of spades and must then decide how to continue. As dummy has just one entry left in the jack of hearts, you can effect only a single spade ruff. So, barring when two spade honours have already come down, playing to ruff the suit good entails relying on a 3-3 break. Since you cannot expect East-West to signal their spade length, you may prefer trying a club to the king. Either way, you need nice things to happen in two suits.

Whilst it slightly increases the chance of losing a trump, you stand a greater chance of success if you finesse West for the heart queen. By doing this you create an extra entry to dummy, which enhances your prospects of enjoying the spades.

After clearing the closed hand's aces, lead a heart to the ten. When East follows low, play a small spade, ruffing in hand, and repeat the trump finesse. Then lead a second low spade and ruff with the heart king. Finally you cross to the ace of trumps, which pulls West's last one, and run the spades. Unless East is 1-2 in the majors, a singleton spade left or right may well beat you no matter who has the ♣A. However you cannot help that.

***Consider how to start a new suit within the context of the hand overall.***

Example 38

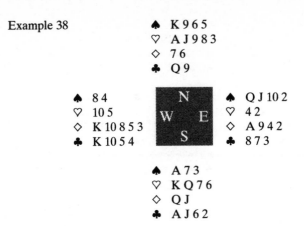

            ♠ K 9 6 5
            ♡ A J 9 8 3
            ◇ 7 6
            ♣ Q 9

♠ 8 4                         ♠ Q J 10 2
♡ 10 5                        ♡ 4 2
◇ K 10 8 5 3                  ◇ A 9 4 2
♣ K 10 5 4                    ♣ 8 7 3

            ♠ A 7 3
            ♡ K Q 7 6
            ◇ Q J
            ♣ A J 6 2

Against your contract of Four Hearts, West starts off with the eight of spades.

Here you can see two fast diamond losers. In addition you may lose a club and the third round of spades belongs to the enemy. How then might you restrict the defence to three tricks?

One option is to take the club finesse, no doubt after drawing trumps. This succeeds when East holds the club king. If not, and someone has length in both black suits, a squeeze might work, though this can be broken up. What other choices exist?

Well, you can play for the king of clubs to lie over the ace. If you start clubs with a small card from hand, West will then face a quandary. Rising with the king allows you to make three clubs in all, and hence to get two spades away from dummy. On the other hand, ducking the first club means the king never scores.

The ♠8 appears to come from a doubleton, which hints that West may have the club king (with no reason to believe you cannot readily draw trumps, your opponent might otherwise have chosen to lead from length rather than try for a ruff; also there is simply more room for West to hold the ♣K). Happily you can improve on just placing West with the card. You should also test this defender's nerve. When you lead a club, plan to stick in the nine if West follows low smoothly. In practice you will thereby fulfil your contract whenever the ten *or* the king sits to your left.

*Defenders rarely withhold honours they may go to bed with later – use this knowledge to your advantage.*

Example 39

Game All
Dealer West

♠ A
♡ K Q 8 6 4
♢ A 6 4 3
♣ A Q 9

| SOUTH | WEST | NORTH | EAST |
|-------|------|--------|------|
|       | 3♠   | Double | Pass |
| 5♢    | Pass | 6♢     | End  |

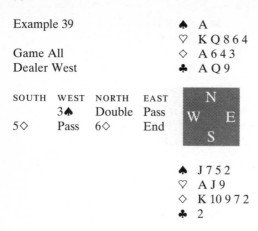

♠ J 7 5 2
♡ A J 9
♢ K 10 9 7 2
♣ 2

West leads the king of spades, which dummy's ace wins.
What looks like the safest line for your excellent slam?

Example 40

Game All
Dealer South

♠ Q 4
♡ A 8 6
♢ J 7 3
♣ 9 8 7 6 3

| SOUTH | WEST | NORTH | EAST |
|--------|--------|-------|------|
| 1♠     | Double | Pass  | 2♢   |
| Double | Pass   | 3♣    | Pass |
| 3♠     | Pass   | 4♠    | End  |

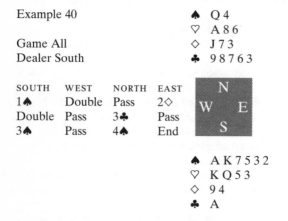

♠ A K 7 5 3 2
♡ K Q 5 3
♢ 9 4
♣ A

West leads the ♢A, East signalling four cards with the eight. Next
comes the club king, which as it happens is not best defence, and your
ace wins.

How do you proceed?

Example 41

♠ A Q 9 7
♡ J 9

East–West game
Dealer South

♦ K 8 7 2
♣ A 10 3

| SOUTH | WEST | NORTH | EAST |
|-------|------|-------|------|
| 1♡ | Pass | 1♠ | Pass |
| 2♣ | Pass | 3NT | Pass |
| 4♣ | Pass | 4♡ | End |

| | N | |
|---|---|---|
| W | | E |
| | S | |

♠ 6 2
♡ A 6 5 4 3 2
♦ —
♣ K Q J 8 7

West leads the queen of diamonds against your game.

Prospects seem bright indeed. How best can you prepare for possible bad breaks?

Example 42

♠ J 8 4 3
♡ Q 6 5

East–West game
Dealer South

♦ 10 7 3 2
♣ 10 2

| SOUTH | WEST | NORTH | EAST |
|-------|------|-------|------|
| 2♣ | Pass | 2♦ | Pass |
| 2♡ | Pass | 4♡ | Pass |
| All Pass | | | |

| | N | |
|---|---|---|
| W | | E |
| | S | |

♠ A 5
♡ A K 7 4 2
♦ Q 4
♣ A K Q 5

West leads the nine of clubs to your ace.

On the assumption that trumps split 3-2 you can count nine tricks. Where will you go for a tenth?

Example 39

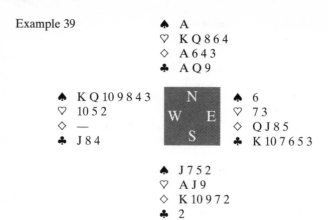

&spades; A
&hearts; K Q 8 6 4
&diams; A 6 4 3
&clubs; A Q 9

&spades; K Q 10 9 8 4 3
&hearts; 10 5 2
&diams; —
&clubs; J 8 4

&spades; 6
&hearts; 7 3
&diams; Q J 8 5
&clubs; K 10 7 6 5 3

&spades; J 7 5 2
&hearts; A J 9
&diams; K 10 9 7 2
&clubs; 2

West, who pre-empted in spades, leads the king of spades against your small slam in diamonds. The ace wins perforce.

The contract looks excellent – indeed a 2-2 trump division will permit you to take all thirteen tricks. A 3-1 split will hardly trouble you either. Even if someone turns up with a heart void, you will have marked finesse after cashing the ace.

With these diamonds, one way to counter four cards on your right is small to the ten, saving the &diams;A to ruff with. Here such a play invites disaster – if West could win the first trump, a second spade would leave you guessing how high to ruff. You would probably ruff high, playing for split honours, and go down if they were both on your left.

Yes, you do want to cater for East having four trumps. Since you cannot safely play up to your ten, you should arrange the next best thing. This is to broach the diamonds by leading the ten from hand. If West follows suit, you can go up with dummy's ace. When West shows out, you let it run round to East's jack.

To enter your hand to lead the &diams;10 you will have to risk West ruffing the first heart as ruffing a club can result in a second trump loser. After East takes the jack of trumps, you win the heart return in hand, ruff a spade high and finesse the seven of diamonds. The club ace serves for an entry to lead diamonds once more and pick up the queen.

***Ensure that taking a safety play in one suit does not expose you to a greater danger elsewhere.***

Example 40

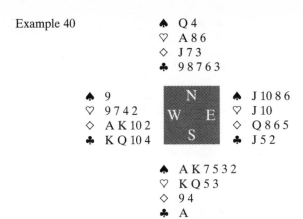

```
              ♠ Q 4
              ♡ A 8 6
              ◇ J 7 3
              ♣ 9 8 7 6 3

 ♠ 9                          ♠ J 10 8 6
 ♡ 9 7 4 2         N          ♡ J 10
 ◇ A K 10 2    W       E      ◇ Q 8 6 5
 ♣ K Q 10 4        S          ♣ J 5 2

              ♠ A K 7 5 3 2
              ♡ K Q 5 3
              ◇ 9 4
              ♣ A
```

You find yourself in Four Spades after West has doubled your opening bid. West leads the ◇A, East signalling four cards with the eight. Next comes the club king (a trump shift beats you, but this is hard to find) and your ace wins.

As on the previous hand, friendly breaks will allow you to record an overtrick. However West's take-out double warns that you may find four or perhaps five hearts on your left and four spades to your right. If this is the layout, you have four losers.

The lack of entries to dummy means that you cannot ruff out the clubs. Squeeze chances also look slim – the opponents can attack your heart entries and East may well guard clubs. So you must devise a safe way to ruff your last heart in dummy.

At trick three, give up a diamond. Once you regain the lead, go over to the ♡A and return the suit. When East follows, you win with the ♡K and cross to the ♠Q. You then lead another heart through East. You are happy if this defender ever ruffs your loser as, thanks to your diamond play, the other cannot get in to give a second ruff. When East discards, you score your heart queen and lead a fourth round. East can overruff the dummy, but you do not mind as it is with a natural trump trick.

Note that if hearts were 5-1, a trump at trick four would beat you. You would have to win in dummy, lead a heart to the king and one back to the ace, whereupon East would ruff. Even so this does not detract from the correctness of the line suggested.

*When you have to play with fire, try to limit the enemy's ruffing options to trumping your losers.*

Example 41

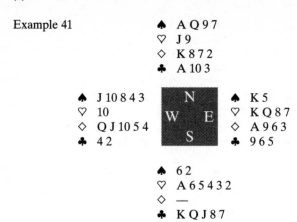

♠ A Q 9 7
♡ J 9
◇ K 8 7 2
♣ A 10 3

♠ J 10 8 4 3
♡ 10
◇ Q J 10 5 4
♣ 4 2

♠ K 5
♡ K Q 8 7
◇ A 9 6 3
♣ 9 6 5

♠ 6 2
♡ A 6 5 4 3 2
◇ —
♣ K Q J 8 7

You are in the sound contract of Four Hearts and West leads the queen of diamonds.

You cannot handle a five nil trump split and a three two break will make the contract a cakewalk. So you work out how best to handle a four one division. If West has underled the ace of diamonds and you put up dummy's king at trick one, you can dispose of a spade loser. Otherwise a successful spade finesse will see you home. Might you also find a way to make the contract when both the key pointed-suit honours sit on your right?

If you throw East in, you can cope with almost anything. On the bidding it is unlikely that anyone would lead away from the ace of diamonds at trick one. Therefore you preserve dummy's ◇K and ruff the queen lead in hand. To minimise the risk of West ruffing a club with a doubleton trump, you next duck a heart. You hope that when in fact West has a singleton trump it is not a picture – you do not want a spade switch through the ace-queen. Happily this is the case. You win the club exit, cash the ace of trumps and then turn back to clubs.

You must now extract East's last two clubs (ending in hand) and cut adrift with a trump. East makes two heart winners (you can spare low spades from dummy) and afterwards attempts to escape with a low diamond. Sticking to your guns, you let this run round to dummy's king, and throw your losing spade away.

*Whenever your losers are slow ones, look to see if there is an effective way to throw an opponent in.*

Example 42

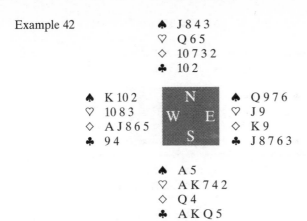

```
            ♠ J 8 4 3
            ♡ Q 6 5
            ◇ 10 7 3 2
            ♣ 10 2
♠ K 10 2                    ♠ Q 9 7 6
♡ 10 8 3       N           ♡ J 9
◇ A J 8 6 5  W   E         ◇ K 9
♣ 9 4          S           ♣ J 8 7 6 3
            ♠ A 5
            ♡ A K 7 4 2
            ◇ Q 4
            ♣ A K Q 5
```

Four Hearts looks less solid this time, but again that is where the auction has come to rest. West leads the nine of clubs to your ace. With such a strong hand, you cannot bear the thought of going minus, can you?

As you face three certain losers in spades and diamonds, you need to play the other suits without loss. Thus you have to presume a 3-2 trump break. Also you will no doubt want to ruff your small club in dummy. How can you accomplish this safely?

With no clue about the enemy clubs, you would cash the ace and queen of hearts before tackling clubs. After that you would play off the ♣K and continue with the five. You would succeed when the defender with three trumps has at least three clubs. Here though you can judge how the opposing clubs may lie . . .

The opening lead of the club nine looks very much like the top of a doubleton. This indicates that if one opponent trumps in, it can only be West. Should such knowledge alter your play?

Think about it. Assuming West started with two clubs to East's five, the third trump rates to turn up on your left. In this case you must conserve North's ♡Q to overruff West. The final two opposing trumps will then fall together. So just cash your ace of hearts before switching to the king and five of clubs.

*There is no hard and fast rule about how many rounds of trumps to draw – consider each case on its own merit.*

Example 43

|  | ♠ | J 8 6 |
|---|---|---|
|  | ♡ | Q 6 2 |

East–West game   ♦ A K 7 6 3
Dealer South   ♣ A K

| SOUTH | WEST | NORTH | EAST |
|---|---|---|---|
| 1♡ | Pass | 3♦ | Pass |
| 3♡ | Pass | 4♣ | Pass |
| 4♠ | Pass | 5♣ | Pass |
| 6♡ | All Pass | | |

N
W E
S

♠ A 7 4 3
♡ A K J 10 9 8
♦ 10 2
♣ 4

An exchange of cue bids enables you to reach the good slam. West leads the jack of clubs.

How do you aim to secure twelve tricks?

Example 44

|  | ♠ | A 6 |
|---|---|---|
|  | ♡ | J 10 9 4 |

Love All   ♦ A 7 6 5
Dealer South   ♣ K 10 3

| SOUTH | WEST | NORTH | EAST |
|---|---|---|---|
| 1♡ | 2♡* | 2♠ | 4♠ |
| Pass | Pass | 5♡ | End |

N
W E
S

♠ 10
* spades and a minor   ♡ A K 7 5 3
♦ 9 4 3 2
♣ A Q 5

Your pass was forcing and North has done well to bid on.

West leads the king of spades, captured by dummy's ace. To cater for a lone queen of trumps, you next lead a heart to the ace, but West pitches the club six.

Can you see the best way to carry on from here?

Example 45

♠ 10 8 6 5 4
♡ K 7

Love All
Dealer East

♢ A 8 7 6 3
♣ 7

| SOUTH | WEST | NORTH | EAST |
|-------|------|-------|------|
|       |      |       | 3♡   |
| 4♢    | Pass | 5♢    | End  |

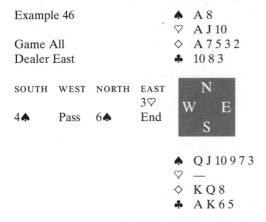

♠ A
♡ 9 4
♢ K Q J 10 2
♣ A K 8 4 2

West leads the ♡J, which you cover with dummy's king. East produces the ace-queen of hearts and shifts to the ♣J. You win it and lay down the ♢K, but West contributes the ♣3.

How can you land what has become a tricky contract?

Example 46

♠ A 8
♡ A J 10

Game All
Dealer East

♢ A 7 5 3 2
♣ 10 8 3

| SOUTH | WEST | NORTH | EAST |
|-------|------|-------|------|
|       |      |       | 3♡   |
| 4♠    | Pass | 6♠    | End  |

♠ Q J 10 9 7 3
♡ —
♢ K Q 8
♣ A K 6 5

West leads the seven of hearts, covered by the ten, queen and ruffed. At trick two you run the queen of spades. East wins this with the king and switches to the four of clubs.

A 3-2 diamond break would render your slam a cinch, so how might you overcome a less helpful layout?

Example 43

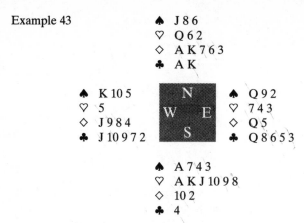

```
              ♠ J 8 6
              ♡ Q 6 2
              ◇ A K 7 6 3
              ♣ A K

  ♠ K 10 5                    ♠ Q 9 2
  ♡ 5            N            ♡ 7 4 3
  ◇ J 9 8 4   W     E         ◇ Q 5
  ♣ J 10 9 7 2    S           ♣ Q 8 6 5 3

              ♠ A 7 4 3
              ♡ A K J 10 9 8
              ◇ 10 2
              ♣ 4
```

You declare Six Hearts and West leads the jack of clubs.

You have eleven top winners and dummy's diamond suit offers great hope for a twelfth. The opening lead has removed one of dummy's entries, but you will have to live with that.

At trick two you ought to cash your trump ace to test that suit. When all follow, you know the ♡Q may provide access to dummy at a vital moment. How can you benefit from this?

You need to score only one of dummy's three low diamonds. This implies that, if you can resolve the entry position, you can handle a 4-2 diamond break. If trumps divide two apiece and cashing the spade ace leaves a defender with a bare spade honour, you can organise an endplay. You will cash the king of hearts and play three rounds of diamonds, ruffing the third, before exiting with a spade. A return of either minor will then enable you to ruff the diamonds good while the queen of hearts stands in dummy. This time though a snazzy line is not best . . .

Simply concede a diamond at trick three. Then you can win a spade or a heart return in your hand (which explains why you did not cash a second trump). You go on to cash the ace of diamonds and ruff a small diamond in your hand. Finally you draw trumps ending in dummy and run the diamonds.

Note that if someone showed out of hearts at trick two, you would draw trumps and duck a diamond hoping they break 3-3.

*On occasion a first-round duck can prove a useful aid in ruffing out a suit.*

Example 44

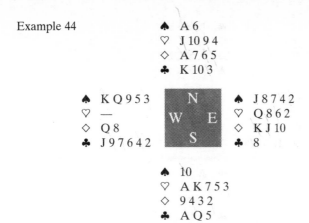

```
              ♠ A 6
              ♡ J 10 9 4
              ◇ A 7 6 5
              ♣ K 10 3
  ♠ K Q 9 5 3              ♠ J 8 7 4 2
  ♡ —            N         ♡ Q 8 6 2
  ◇ Q 8       W   E        ◇ K J 10
  ♣ J 9 7 6 4 2   S        ♣ 8
              ♠ 10
              ♡ A K 7 5 3
              ◇ 9 4 3 2
              ♣ A Q 5
```

East-West bid to 4♠, which pushes you into 5♡.

West leads the king of spades, captured by dummy's ace. You next lead a heart to the ace. The queen does not drop, indeed West pitches the club six.

On a 2-2 trump split, you could strip the hand and duck a diamond, so combating any West stiff bar the eight. Now you must rely on 3-2 diamonds. Still you must tread carefully.

Drawing all the trumps will result in certain defeat. To set up a fourth-round diamond winner you must lose the lead twice. With only *one* heart left, you cannot trump *two* spades.

Leaving three trumps at large fails too. You can spare your long heart on the next spade, but what about the one after that? Ruffing in dummy will help promote East's eight. Likewise, if you ruff in hand, you will lack the length required to pick up the queen. To solve this riddle you have to put your opponent on the spot.

Cross to the diamond ace at trick three and lead two heart honours through East. If they hold, dummy can take one spade force. If one is covered, you will be able to accept both spade taps in the closed hand. Whatever happens, you will have time to establish a long diamond. Finally the clubs will allow you to get wherever you need to be to pull the last trump.

***If you lead through a defender's strength then you can adjust your play to suit.***

80

Example 45

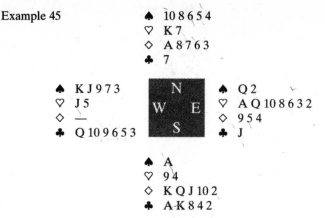

```
              ♠ 10 8 6 5 4
              ♡ K 7
              ◇ A 8 7 6 3
              ♣ 7

  ♠ K J 9 7 3        N         ♠ Q 2
  ♡ J 5          W       E     ♡ A Q 10 8 6 3 2
  ◇ —                          ◇ 9 5 4
  ♣ Q 10 9 6 5 3     S         ♣ J

              ♠ A
              ♡ 9 4
              ◇ K Q J 10 2
              ♣ A K 8 4 2
```

East deals and opens 3♡. Thereafter you reach game in diamonds, from what quickly looks like the wrong way up.

West leads the jack of hearts, which you decide to cover with the king. East produces the ace-queen of hearts and shifts to the jack of clubs. You capture that with the ace, West following with the five. Next you lay down the king of diamonds, but West contributes the ♣3.

Now you reckon on only two safe club ruffs; they can wait for a minute. These winners, plus five trump tricks and three black suit tops, will give you ten in total. If West began with five clubs, your last club will become good, but who would be in a hurry to throw a club from five? This factor inclines you to read the hand on your left for a 5-2-0-6 shape.

To fulfil your contract you need to exert pressure on West, who holds length in both black suits. Moreover, with ruffing menaces in each black suit, a squeeze will bite quite early – to be precise, on the third trump.

To make the position fluid for ruffing in either hand, you next unblock the ace of spades. When you go on to cash the queen of diamonds West pitches a spade. After that you continue with the jack, a key move as it allows you to choose where to win this, the squeeze trick. Let us study the cards remaining in play at such a crucial moment:

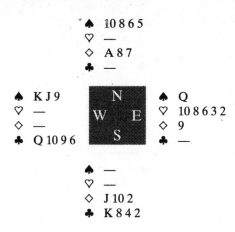

```
               ♠ 10 8 6 5
               ♡ —
               ◇ A 8 7
               ♣ —

   ♠ K J 9         N          ♠ Q
   ♡ —        W         E     ♡ 10 8 6 3 2
   ◇ —                        ◇ 9
   ♣ Q 10 9 6       S         ♣ —

               ♠ —
               ♡ —
               ◇ J 10 2
               ♣ K 8 4 2
```

If West releases another club, you allow the jack to hold and ruff the clubs good. Instead the defender may let a spade go. In that case you overtake your jack of diamonds with dummy's ace. With the lead in the right place, you trump two spades in your hand to set up a long card in that suit. Oh boy!

Before moving to the next deal, do you want to know what might happen on this one if West fished out a spade as the opening lead? Then you could not transpose to the position laid out above. If you tried conceding two heart tricks (essential to bring your opponent under pressure), East could take those and play a second spade. This would destroy the entry-shifting squeeze. For instance, if you ruffed the spade and proceeded to lead three high trumps, West could spare one card from each black suit and then a club.

On an initial spade attack you should cash two rounds of trumps finishing in dummy. Then ruff a spade to hand, lead out your high clubs (throwing a spade from dummy) and crossruff the black suits. East can score the diamond nine on an overruff or by trumping one of your big clubs. However, having gained the lead, East will have to concede a trick to the king of hearts.

*You may solve an entry shortage in a squeeze ending by giving yourself a choice of where to win the squeeze trick.*

Example 46

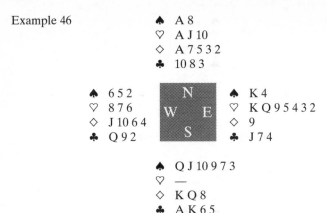

```
                    ♠  A 8
                    ♡  A J 10
                    ◇  A 7 5 3 2
                    ♣  10 8 3

   ♠  6 5 2            N           ♠  K 4
   ♡  8 7 6                        ♡  K Q 9 5 4 3 2
   ◇  J 10 6 4     W       E       ◇  9
   ♣  Q 9 2            S           ♣  J 7 4

                    ♠  Q J 10 9 7 3
                    ♡  —
                    ◇  K Q 8
                    ♣  A K 6 5
```

Again East opens Three Hearts and this time you arrive in Six Spades. West leads the seven of hearts, covered by the ten, queen and ruffed. At trick two you run the queen of spades. East wins this with the king and switches to the four of clubs.

If diamonds divide 3-2, all will be plain sailing, but East's 3♡ bid warns of bad breaks. As dummy lacks a suitable late entry, ruffing out the diamonds would get you nowhere. You therefore conclude that on a 4-1 split you will require a squeeze.

East alone can look after the jack of hearts and you predict West will guard the diamonds. Since both defenders may be able to stop clubs, you should prepare for a double squeeze.

Suppose you simply put up your ace of clubs, unblock the spades, cross to your diamond king and pull the missing trump. Then continue by cashing the queen of diamonds and running the trumps. No, this sequence is not going to work – what can dummy pitch from ♡A-J, ◇A-7 and the ♣10 on the last spade? Both hearts are needed to keep a threat against East. Likewise the diamonds have to stay there to retain a menace in that suit. Of course the club is vital too, allowing you to get back to the ace and a possible long card if both defenders abandon clubs.

Before returning to hand, you must clear the heart ace out of dummy, pitching your ♣5. Then come back to the diamond king, draw West's trump and lead your other high diamond to test the suit.

These cards remain:

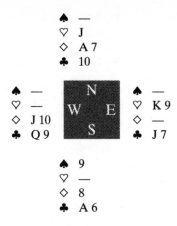

```
              ♠  —
              ♡  J
              ◇  A 7
              ♣  10

  ♠  —        ┌─────────┐      ♠  —
  ♡  —        │    N    │      ♡  K 9
  ◇  J 10     │  W   E  │      ◇  —
  ♣  Q 9      │    S    │      ♣  J 7
              └─────────┘
              ♠  9
              ♡  —
              ◇  8
              ♣  A 6
```

Now when you play the last trump, West has to release a club to keep the diamonds stopped. As you took care to play a second round of diamonds earlier and have seen East show out, you know the ◇7 will not win. So, its job done, you throw it from dummy on this trick.

Finally you go over to the diamond ace, finishing off East in the process. Depending on that defender's choice of discard, either your low club or dummy's heart jack will become good.

Note how much less stringent conditions would have been if East had not attacked clubs when in with the trump king. Your second master club would have given dummy a spare card. You could have just run all your trumps throwing two clubs and a diamond from dummy. At the end you would have taken the red suit tops, not caring which defender was squeezed first.

As a point of defence, attacking entries in the suit that both defenders can guard often proves effective in breaking up a double squeeze. However, on the example here such a strategy would fail.

Suppose West starts off with the two of clubs. Then the eight in dummy brings forth East's jack, leaving West exposed to a simple squeeze in the minors. If West finds the inspired lead of the club queen, declarer can counter by letting East's later club return run round to the ten. The defence would need better spot cards in clubs to stand a real chance.

***Picturing why a squeeze ending might go wrong will help you set it up correctly.***

Example 47

North–South game
Dealer West

|  | ♠ | A 7 5 3 |
|---|---|---|
|  | ♡ | A Q 10 6 |
|  | ◇ | 5 |
|  | ♣ | Q J 4 3 |

| SOUTH | WEST | NORTH | EAST |
|---|---|---|---|
|  | 2◇* | Double | Pass |
| 3◇ | Pass | 4◇ | Pass |
| 4NT | Pass | 5♡ | Pass |
| 6♠ | All Pass |  |  |

*weak

|  | ♠ | K Q 8 2 |
|---|---|---|
|  | ♡ | K J 5 3 |
|  | ◇ | K Q 10 6 |
|  | ♣ | A |

West leads the ♠10. Assuming trumps break 3-2 you can get up to eleven tricks by taking one ruff in either hand.

Where do you look for a twelfth?

Example 48

Love All
Dealer South

|  | ♠ | Q 10 6 3 |
|---|---|---|
|  | ♡ | A 9 6 |
|  | ◇ | A 7 |
|  | ♣ | Q 8 4 3 |

| SOUTH | WEST | NORTH | EAST |
|---|---|---|---|
| 1♠ | 2NT | 3♣* | Pass |
| 3♠ | Pass | 4♠ | End |

* value raise in spades

|  | ♠ | A 8 7 5 4 2 |
|---|---|---|
|  | ♡ | K 8 2 |
|  | ◇ | J 2 |
|  | ♣ | K 7 |

West, who has shown at least five-five in the minors, leads the king of diamonds. East plays the five under the ace. You decide to lead a spade to your ace at trick two, which collects the jack from East and the nine from West.

How do you proceed?

Example 49                  ♠ 9 5

                       ♡ Q 9 5 2

Game All               ♢ A 8 4

Dealer South          ♣ K Q 9 3

| SOUTH | WEST | NORTH | EAST |
|---|---|---|---|
| 2♣ | Pass | 2NT | Pass |
| 3♠ | Pass | 3NT | Pass |
| 4♠ | Pass | 5♢* | Pass |
| 6♠ | Double | All Pass | |

                  ♠ A K 10 7 6 4 2

\* cue bid          ♡ —

                  ♢ K Q J 7

                  ♣ A 4

After a strong-sounding sequence West's double comes as a surprise. You soon discover the reason behind it. After ruffing the ace of hearts lead, you lay down the ace of spades only to find East putting another heart on the table.

How do you recover?

Example 50                ♠ K 8 3

                     ♡ Q 10 6 2

Love All               ♢ Q 7 6 4

Dealer South          ♣ K 5

| SOUTH | WEST | NORTH | EAST |
|---|---|---|---|
| 1♡ | Pass | 3♡ | Pass |
| 4♡ | All Pass | | |

                  ♠ Q 10 6

                  ♡ A K J 9 3

                  ♢ 5 3

                  ♣ A 10 4

The opening lead is the six of clubs.

How can you give this contract a really good chance?

Example 47

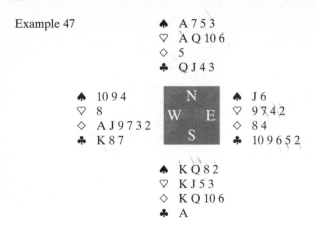

```
                    ♠  A 7 5 3
                    ♡  A Q 10 6
                    ◇  5
                    ♣  Q J 4 3

    ♠  10 9 4          N          ♠  J 6
    ♡  8                          ♡  9 7 4 2
    ◇  A J 9 7 3 2  W     E       ◇  8 4
    ♣  K 8 7           S          ♣  10 9 6 5 2

                    ♠  K Q 8 2
                    ♡  K J 5 3
                    ◇  K Q 10 6
                    ♣  A
```

West, who has opened a weak 2◇, leads the ten of trumps against your little slam in spades. Your first thought is that with the ace of diamonds a sure loser you must assume the trumps play without loss. Of course that still leaves you a trick short.

Although you can easily take one ruff in either hand, you really want two. There is also the ruffing club finesse to try, or East just might hold a diamond honour.

To trump diamonds you rise with the spade ace and play to your king of diamonds. After West wins with the ace, you take one more round of trumps with your king. Thereafter you ruff two diamonds in dummy, hoping East has no more trumps and so cannot overruff. This happens to work, but you should reject it.

Conversely, to ruff two clubs you win the first trick in hand. You will later need to cross to dummy twice in hearts, which the way the cards lie allows West to ruff in. Playing East for minor suit honours involves risk as well. So which line is the safest?

As the bidding almost marks the ace of diamonds on your left, you should go for an endplay. Draw trumps, unblock the ♣A and next cash the king, jack and ace of hearts. Then lead a diamond to the king. If West ducks, you cross to the queen of hearts and drive out the ♣K. Otherwise West is on play and must give you a free finesse.

*The bidding can both warn which lines of play may fail and point you towards the winning strategy.*

Example 48

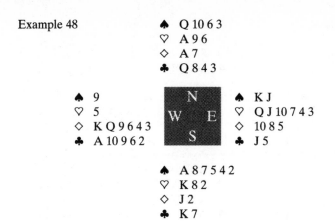

```
              ♠ Q 10 6 3
              ♡ A 9 6
              ◇ A 7
              ♣ Q 8 4 3

♠ 9                           ♠ K J
♡ 5               N           ♡ Q J 10 7 4 3
◇ K Q 9 6 4 3   W   E         ◇ 10 8 5
♣ A 10 9 6 2      S           ♣ J 5

              ♠ A 8 7 5 4 2
              ♡ K 8 2
              ◇ J 2
              ♣ K 7
```

West, who has shown a minor two-suiter, starts with the king of diamonds in defence to your contract of Four Spades. East plays the five under the ace. At trick two you decide to lead a spade to your ace, which collects the jack from East and the nine from West. How should you continue?

At first sight this one seems easy – cash the ace-king of hearts and put West on play with a diamond. To avoid giving you a ruff and discard, this defender must then exit in clubs. That ought to allow both your king and North's queen to score.

Suddenly the awful truth hits you. Unless West underleads the ace of clubs, you cannot reach dummy in time. Oh dear!

You can instead play the hand on your left for six clubs and hope to endplay your other opponent. You give up a diamond, win the heart return in hand and sneak a club through. Later you put East in with the third heart.

For two reasons you tend to place West with six diamonds rather than six clubs. East's five spot at trick one looks low and the same player's failure to interject Three Diamonds speaks volumes too. In any case the best line wins against shapes of 2-1-5-5, 1-1-6-5 and 1-1-5-6.

Simply cash the king of hearts and then cut loose with a diamond. The enforced club exit sets up two tricks for you in the suit, whilst the ace of hearts stands ready as an entry.

*Two-suited bids can tell you much about the unseen hands – ensure you make the most of this.*

Example 49

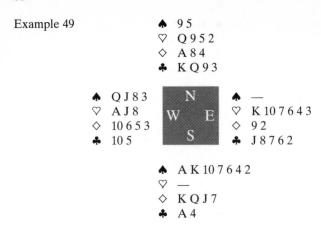

```
                    ♠  9 5
                    ♡  Q 9 5 2
                    ◇  A 8 4
                    ♣  K Q 9 3

    ♠  Q J 8 3         N         ♠  —
    ♡  A J 8      W         E    ♡  K 10 7 6 4 3
    ◇  10 6 5 3                  ◇  9 2
    ♣  10 5            S         ♣  J 8 7 6 2

                    ♠  A K 10 7 6 4 2
                    ♡  —
                    ◇  K Q J 7
                    ♣  A 4
```

You bid to Six Spades and soon discover why West has doubled. After ruffing the ace of hearts lead, you lay down the trump ace only to find East putting another heart on the table.

As your left-hand opponent appears to have two natural trump winners, nothing except a trump endplay offers hope of salvation. To force a trump return, you will need to clear out West's plain cards before exiting with a low spade. You can use dummy's two entries to ruff two more hearts in hand, which means you require West to have started with three hearts.

Although you have seven minor-suit winners, you need just six. This provides you with a choice of plays. If West was dealt a 4-3-3-3 shape, you want to score three club tricks, pitching a diamond on the third. When West holds a 4-3-4-2, you must take four diamonds but only two clubs.

To ensure all your options remain open, cash the king and queen of diamonds at tricks three and four. Now when you cross to North's ace, East shows out. So next you trump a heart and cash the ◇J followed by the club ace. Then cross to the ♣K and ruff another heart to hand. Finally you advance a small spade to leave West feeling far from happy: on any lead bar a heart you could only succeed by leaving trumps alone and ruffing the fourth diamond to gain an extra entry. Without a double you would never take that line, and probably not with it.

***When the success of a given line depends on a defender having a specific shape, aim to get at least a partial count.***

Example 50

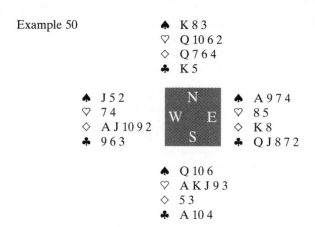

♠ K 8 3
♡ Q 10 6 2
♢ Q 7 6 4
♣ K 5

♠ J 5 2
♡ 7 4
♢ A J 10 9 2
♣ 9 6 3

♠ A 9 7 4
♡ 8 5
♢ K 8
♣ Q J 8 7 2

♠ Q 10 6
♡ A K J 9 3
♢ 5 3
♣ A 10 4

A simple auction brings you to the heart game. The opening lead is the six of clubs and you study your prospects.

Since two diamonds and one spade must be lost, you will have to avoid conceding a second spade. You can start on that suit from your hand, which will enable you to pick up ace-jack doubleton on your left. You would also prevail if East holds the jack of spades. What other chances can you give yourself?

You presume that holding the ace-king or the jack-ten of diamonds West would have preferred to lead a diamond at trick one. Therefore, rather than leading up to dummy's diamond queen, you will duck a couple of rounds. If you find ♢A-K-10 alone on your right, you can set up a fourth-round winner via a ruff. Might ducking a diamond yield another benefit?

Yes, if trumps divide 2-2 and you strip the hand first, tackling diamonds may endplay the enemy. Draw trumps and play three rounds of clubs, ruffing the third. This way if East holds honour doubleton diamond or West possesses ♢A-J or ♢K-J stiff, the defence will have to break open the spades. Unless East leads spades and West has the ace-jack-nine of the suit, this will enable you to play them for one loser (possibly with a guess). As the cards lie East will lead the four and West will play the jack on your six, which resolves the spades without further ado.

***Many holdings lend themselves to a throw in – seek and ye shall find.***

90

Example 51

♠ 8 7 6 2
♡ K 8 7 3
♦ J 4
♣ K 10 9

East–West game
Dealer South

| SOUTH | WEST | NORTH | EAST |
|-------|------|-------|------|
| 1♠ | Double | 3♠ | Pass |
| 4♠ | All Pass | | |

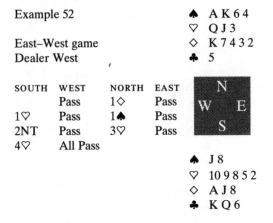

♠ A K Q J 10 9
♡ Q 5 4
♦ Q
♣ A 8 3

West tries two top diamonds, East giving a gentle echo with the six and five. You ruff the second and draw the opposing trumps in two rounds, West pitching the ◇3.

How do you proceed?

Example 52

♠ A K 6 4
♡ Q J 3
♦ K 7 4 3 2
♣ 5

East–West game
Dealer West

| SOUTH | WEST | NORTH | EAST |
|-------|------|-------|------|
| | Pass | 1♦ | Pass |
| 1♡ | Pass | 1♠ | Pass |
| 2NT | Pass | 3♡ | Pass |
| 4♡ | All Pass | | |

♠ J 8
♡ 10 9 8 5 2
♦ A J 8
♣ K Q 6

West starts off with the two of clubs, which East takes with the ace. Next come a low heart to the king, one back to the ace and a third round of trumps. West discards the seven of clubs on this.

How are you going to avoid a diamond loser?

Example 53                          ♠  A Q 8 2
                                    ♡  A 6 5
Love All                            ◇  A K 2
Dealer East                         ♣  A 9 4

| SOUTH | WEST | NORTH | EAST | |
|-------|------|-------|------|---|
|       |      |       | Pass | |
| 4◇    | Double | Rdbl | Pass | |
| Pass  | 4♠   | 7◇    | End  | |

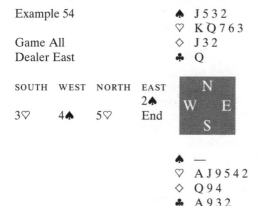

                                    ♠  —
                                    ♡  9 4
                                    ◇  Q J 10 8 7 6 5 4
                                    ♣  K 8 2

A spirited auction lands you at the wheel in an exciting grand slam.
West leads the ♡K to the ace, jack and four.

Since you cannot take the spade finesse, you will require a squeeze
of some sort. What ending do you envisage?

Example 54                          ♠  J 5 3 2
                                    ♡  K Q 7 6 3
Game All                            ◇  J 3 2
Dealer East                         ♣  Q

| SOUTH | WEST | NORTH | EAST | |
|-------|------|-------|------|---|
|       |      |       | 2♠   | |
| 3♡    | 4♠   | 5♡    | End  | |

                                    ♠  —
                                    ♡  A J 9 5 4 2
                                    ◇  Q 9 4
                                    ♣  A 9 3 2

After a lively battle you win the contract at the five level. West leads
the six of spades to East's ace and you ruff.

You play a trump and both defenders will follow.

What is your line?

Example 51

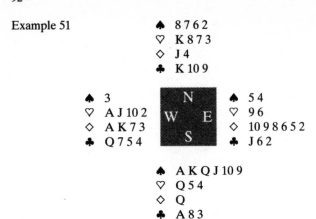

```
                    ♠ 8 7 6 2
                    ♡ K 8 7 3
                    ◇ J 4
                    ♣ K 10 9

    ♠ 3                         ♠ 5 4
    ♡ A J 10 2        N         ♡ 9 6
    ◇ A K 7 3      W     E      ◇ 10 9 8 6 5 2
    ♣ Q 7 5 4         S         ♣ J 6 2

                    ♠ A K Q J 10 9
                    ♡ Q 5 4
                    ◇ Q
                    ♣ A 8 3
```

West, who doubled your 1♠ opener, tries two top diamonds against your game contract in the suit. You ruff the second (noting that East probably has an even number) and draw the opposing trumps in two rounds, West pitching the ◇3.

You expect West to hold the heart ace, but this is unlikely to be a doubleton. So, seeing two heart losers, you cannot afford to lose a club as well. If hearts are 3-3, you can set up a long card to dispose of a club. What extra chances can you picture?

If West holds any five clubs, or ♣Q-J-x-(x), you might give up two hearts to arrange a rounded-suit squeeze. Instead you could hope West has ♡A-J-10-9-(x): lead low from hand and duck when West splits honours to leave the defender on play. Happily there is a better option for using your heart spots . . .

By advancing your queen you oblige West to take the ace and exit with a low heart. Unless this opponent possesses the strong suit cited above, or hearts are 3-3, holding back North's ♡K will then endplay East into leading a club. On the likely low club exit you clobber West's honour with dummy's king.

You now have a better line than the squeeze – the hand on your left cannot have a spade, four hearts, four diamonds *and* five clubs. Best is to next cash the ♡K to test for an even split. When that fails you finesse East for the second club picture.

Yes, West may elect to try a high heart back at trick six, but then you score two heart tricks by force.

***If you manage to block the defence's holding in one suit, a helpful return in another may result.***

Example 52

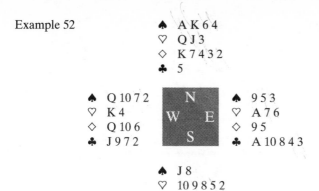

                    ♠  A K 6 4
                    ♡  Q J 3
                    ◇  K 7 4 3 2
                    ♣  5

  ♠  Q 10 7 2              ♠  9 5 3
  ♡  K 4                   ♡  A 7 6
  ◇  Q 10 6               ◇  9 5
  ♣  J 9 7 2              ♣  A 10 8 4 3

                    ♠  J 8
                    ♡  10 9 8 5 2
                    ◇  A J 8
                    ♣  K Q 6

You are in Four Hearts. West starts off with the two of clubs, which East takes with the ace. Next come a low heart to the king, one back to the ace and a third round of trumps. West discards the ♣7 on this. You now need the rest of the tricks.

After first cashing the ◇K to cater for a lone queen offside, you could finesse East for the queen. Instead you might bash down the top two diamonds, hoping the queen drops doubleton, but the odds on this are worse. What else can you play for?

Since only one defender can match dummy's spade length, you could try for a spade-diamond squeeze. It would bite when someone holds four spades together with the guarded queen of diamonds. In addition you would succeed if the ◇Q started life as a doubleton. Furthermore, from the way the early tricks have gone, it looks like West may indeed possess a 4-2-3-4 shape.

So play the ace-king of spades and ruff the third round. Then lead your club winners and last trump, pitching diamonds from dummy. As West has to release a diamond, the queen tumbles down when you cash the king and ace of the suit.

Award yourself a star mark if you spotted a different timing that amounts to the same thing. Unblock the ♡Q-J and win the third heart in hand. Then cash the ♣K-Q and a heart, pitching three diamonds, and finish with three rounds of spades.

*A squeeze can often provide a neat way to combine your chances with an honour dropping of its own accord.*

Example 53

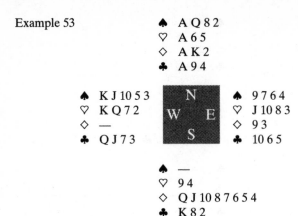

```
              ♠ A Q 8 2
              ♡ A 6 5
              ◇ A K 2
              ♣ A 9 4

  ♠ K J 10 5 3      N        ♠ 9 7 6 4
  ♡ K Q 7 2     W       E    ♡ J 10 8 3
  ◇ —                        ◇ 9 3
  ♣ Q J 7 3         S        ♣ 10 6 5

              ♠ —
              ♡ 9 4
              ◇ Q J 10 8 7 6 5 4
              ♣ K 8 2
```

After West has made a take-out of diamonds and shown a preference for spades, you arrive in Seven Diamonds. West leads the ♡K to the ace, jack and four.

If only you could take the spade finesse, you would have thirteen tricks. Seeing that you cannot do so, you plan for a squeeze. You may well want to get out a pack of cards here!

You can deduce from the play to the first trick that both defenders can guard hearts, and this makes things awkward. You cannot bring off a compound squeeze (cf., example 25) since, with the ace gone from dummy, neither potential heart threat has an entry.

If West has at least five clubs or ♣Q-J-10-(x), you can effect a simple squeeze. Running an avalanche of trumps will leave this opponent unable to retain parity with your clubs at the same time as keeping the spade king guarded. Luckily, thanks to your eight and nine of clubs, you need not rely on that.

Watch what happens when you run your trumps.

West can easily spare two hearts and one club. In addition, given the spade layout and the shortage of late entries to the table, West can afford to release three spades.

Here are the probable cards left at the point you lead your next to last trump:

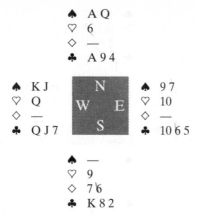

```
              ♠  A Q
              ♡  6
              ◇  —
              ♣  A 9 4

   ♠  K J          N          ♠  9 7
   ♡  Q       W         E     ♡  10
   ◇  —                       ◇  —
   ♣  Q J 7         S         ♣  10 6 5

              ♠  —
              ♡  9
              ◇  7 6
              ♣  K 8 2
```

On this trick West is triple squeezed. Baring the spade king spells defeat and throwing the ♡Q sets up a double squeeze: to keep the ♠K protected West has to let a club go on the final trump, leaving East in sole charge of clubs and hearts. After that going over to the ♣A and cashing the ♠A finishes East.

So in the above position West chucks the club seven, which may save the day if East has ♣10-8-x. You unblock dummy's nine, paving the way for a guard squeeze (or you could throw North's idle heart this time and maybe the ♣9 next).

Your eighth diamond inflicts pressure on West once more. A further club discard would allow you to make the black aces and close by finessing the eight of clubs (hence the earlier unblock). Perhaps then West releases a heart. For your finale you cross to the ♣A and lead the spade ace to polish off East.

Note that the squeeze very likely works if early on you cash the ace of spades, throwing a heart from hand. North's six of hearts functions as a menace instead of your nine. The main thing to stay alert for is that on your final diamond you will need to discard dummy's spade queen unless it has become good.

The possible flaw with using the six as a threat is that the defenders might save the ♠K, the ♡7(!) and four clubs for the last three tricks. Not knowing where that heart is, you could not be sure whether West had started with ♣Q-J-10-x-x. In that case finessing the eight of clubs at trick twelve could backfire.

***When you lack the entries for a routine type of squeeze, look for a suit with good spot cards as a finesse threat.***

Example 54

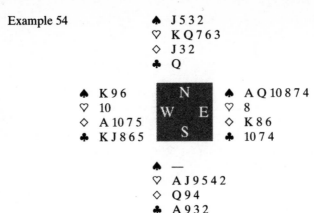

♠ J 5 3 2
♡ K Q 7 6 3
♢ J 3 2
♣ Q

♠ K 9 6          ♠ A Q 10 8 7 4
♡ 10             ♡ 8
♢ A 10 7 5       ♢ K 8 6
♣ K J 8 6 5      ♣ 10 7 4

♠ —
♡ A J 9 5 4 2
♢ Q 9 4
♣ A 9 3 2

After East has opened a weak Two Spades and West has raised to game, you win the contract in Five Hearts. West leads the six of spades to East's ace and you ruff. One round of hearts draws trumps and you plan how to continue.

No matter where the second trick is won you can cross ruff. You trump three more spades in hand and, after cashing the club ace, three clubs in dummy. This enables you to accrue ten tricks in all. Moreover you strip the black suits and gain a full count in the process. Let us now consider the four-card ending.

You can see ♢Q-9-4 and a trump in hand facing ♢J-3-2 and a trump in dummy. The defenders might still hold the rest of the diamonds and they must have the odd black card.

If West has shown up with a 3-1-5-4 or 3-1-2-7 shape, you can claim. In the former case you lead the queen of diamonds (or up to this card). Playing low to (or leading) the jack ensures success in the latter. What though if West is 3-1-4-5 or 3-1-3-6?

The threat of a ruff and discard does not guarantee success now. As a result, you must think who is likely to hold the ♢10. Given that nobody led the suit or doubled, you expect to find the ace and king of diamonds divided. So whoever holds four cards in the suit rates to have the ten. When West does, you exit with the queen of diamonds and let the return run around to your nine. Otherwise you play the jack of diamonds, thereafter finessing the nine.

***Other things being equal, whichever opponent has more cards in any given suit is favourite to hold a key card in it.***

# 3. Bonus Selection

In the time since I worked out what pieces to cover in the first two chapters I have collected a fair amount of fresh material. I present the best of this here by way of a bonus selection.

You may want to ask if I have any personal favourites and I am happy to oblige. I echo the reply of a disc jockey who was asked what tunes on his show he preferred: 'I like them all, that is why I play them'. Having said that, the ones I enjoy most are those combining an original theme with first-class play on both sides and grace and elegance in the key moves.

In the bonus set 66 and 67 stand out as do the final duo. In the main group I have to pick out examples 23, 27 and 51. Each of these are pure constructions, not based at all on hands that I have either played or read about.

A few of the deals in this chapter you may find tricky, all the more so with only two hands in view. However, do not succumb to the temptation of skipping straight to the solution. Instead use the clues from the bidding and early tricks to begin forming a picture of the defenders' hands. Then play devil's advocate: if only one lie of the cards can trouble you, assume it exists; if certain good things need to happen to give you any chance, presume that they will. Top players employ these techniques routinely, which may explain how they sometimes seem to see through the backs of the cards.

Example 55

♠ Q 10 2
♡ K J 6 3

Game All
♢ 10 9

Dealer South
♣ K J 8 2

| SOUTH | WEST | NORTH | EAST |
|-------|------|-------|------|
| 1NT   | Pass | 2♣    | Pass |
| 2♢    | Pass | 3NT   | End  |

♠ A K 6
♡ A 7 2
♢ J 8 7 3 2
♣ A 5

A strong no-trump, Stayman enquiry and denial see you reach the normal no-trump game. West leads the ten of clubs, which should be top of a sequence or interior sequence.

How do you plan the play?

Example 56

♠ A K 7 6
♡ 6

Love All
♢ K Q 10 8

Dealer North
♣ Q J 10 5

| SOUTH | WEST | NORTH | EAST |
|-------|------|-------|------|
|       |      | 1♣    | 2♡*  |
| 2NT   | Pass | 3NT   | End  |

*weak

♠ J 8 3
♡ Q 7 3
♢ A J 9
♣ A 9 7 4

West tables the five of hearts. East wins the first trick with the king of hearts and returns the jack.

What assessment do you make on this hand?

Example 57

North–South game
Dealer South

♠ A K Q 4
♡ K 9 5
◇ 10 7 5
♣ Q 4 2

| SOUTH | WEST | NORTH | EAST |
|-------|------|-------|------|
| 1◇ | Pass | 1♠ | Pass |
| 1NT | Pass | 3NT | End |

♠ 7 6
♡ A J 7
◇ A Q 9 8 3
♣ K 5 3

You conduct a natural sequence to 3NT. West leads the eight of clubs.

How do you plan the play?

Example 58

East–West game
Dealer North

♠ A 9 3
♡ 7 6 5 4
◇ A K Q 3
♣ A 10

| SOUTH | WEST | NORTH | EAST |
|-------|------|-------|------|
|  |  | 1◇ | Pass |
| 1NT | Pass | 2NT | Pass |
| 3NT | All Pass |  |  |

♠ Q 4 2
♡ K J
◇ 8 2
♣ K 8 6 4 3 2

West leads the two of hearts, which East wins with the ace. The nine comes back and your king perforce takes that.

How should you continue?

Example 55

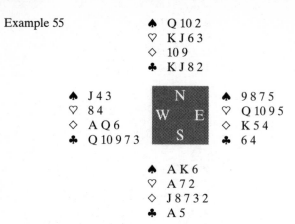

♠ Q 10 2
♡ K J 6 3
◇ 10 9
♣ K J 8 2

♠ J 4 3
♡ 8 4
◇ A Q 6
♣ Q 10 9 7 3

♠ 9 8 7 5
♡ Q 10 9 5
◇ K 5 4
♣ 6 4

♠ A K 6
♡ A 7 2
◇ J 8 7 3 2
♣ A 5

Having denied a four-card major, you reach 3NT and West leads the ten of clubs.

You can count seven sure winners and prospects in three suits for more. What else strikes you on this hand?

With the opponents playing standard leads, you can place West with the nine of clubs but cannot tell who has the queen. Either way a third club trick must be possible, although that still leaves you one short.

If the hearts divide evenly and the finesse works, that suit can produce four tricks. If only one of those things happen, it can yield three. Diamonds look your best bet. Once the top three honours have gone, your remaining cards will be good.

Next you consider whether the opponents might score five tricks before you have time to enjoy the diamonds. Well, yes if you call for dummy's jack at trick one attempting to pick up East's queen. As the cards lie, the jack will hold and East will jump in on the first round of diamonds to continue clubs. You will have to play your ace, leaving West with the queen-nine as equals to knock out the king. With this same defender holding two further entries the enemy will prevail.

If you duck the first trick, a heart switch could beat you. So win with the ace in hand, keeping the king-jack-eight in dummy. Now time is on your side.

***Beware of making a reflex cover of the opening lead – first think about the hand as a whole.***

Example 56

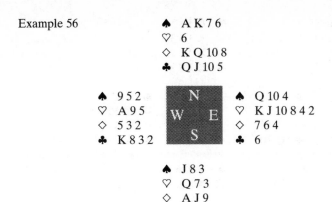

```
              ♠ A K 7 6
              ♡ 6
              ◇ K Q 10 8
              ♣ Q J 10 5

   ♠ 9 5 2              ♠ Q 10 4
   ♡ A 9 5     N        ♡ K J 10 8 4 2
   ◇ 5 3 2   W   E      ◇ 7 6 4
   ♣ K 8 3 2    S       ♣ 6

              ♠ J 8 3
              ♡ Q 7 3
              ◇ A J 9
              ♣ A 9 7 4
```

After East has made a weak jump overcall of Two Hearts you declare 3NT. West leads the five of hearts, won by East's king (yes, sticking in the ten works better for the defence). The jack of hearts return now confronts you.

You can see six certain winners between diamonds and spades. The club suit can provide at least three tricks, four if the king is onside. Thus finding nine tricks should cause no worries. Your problem lies in shutting out the hearts.

You could cover the jack with the queen. West's five spot might have been lowest from three to the ten or middle from three small cards. If East has no sure entry, it would indeed be good defence to underlead the ace, thereby leaving West with another heart to lead later. Do you then put up your queen?

If the queen holds, you will have eight tricks and will surely try to get the ninth without losing the lead. So you will cash two spades in case the queen drops before taking the club finesse.

Most of the time, going up with the queen only brings joy if East began with ace-king-jack of hearts and the king of clubs. That sounds like an awful lot of high cards for a non-vulnerable pre-emptive bid. In any event the heart length marked on your right makes the other hand favourite to hold the club king.

You do better to play West for the ace of hearts. By ducking at trick two you block the opposing hearts. Whether or not West takes the ace, the expected 6-3 break in the suit blocks it.

*If one defender holds three cards to an honour in the other's long suit, look for a chance to create a blockage.*

Example 57

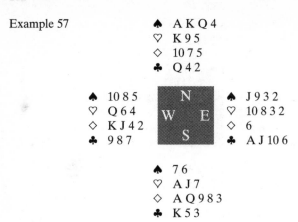

```
                        ♠ A K Q 4
                        ♡ K 9 5
                        ◇ 10 7 5
                        ♣ Q 4 2

        ♠ 10 8 5                        ♠ J 9 3 2
        ♡ Q 6 4          N              ♡ 10 8 3 2
        ◇ K J 4 2     W     E           ◇ 6
        ♣ 9 8 7          S              ♣ A J 10 6

                        ♠ 7 6
                        ♡ A J 7
                        ◇ A Q 9 8 3
                        ♣ K 5 3
```

You are in 3NT once more. West leads the eight of clubs.

A quick count of potential winners looks promising. The majors must give a minimum of five, one club is certain and the diamonds will produce at least three even if both finesses fail.

As on the previous hand, you focus on not losing five tricks before you can score nine. West may have led from ♣A-J-9-8-x or similar. In that case you require only one friendly position in the red suits. You can win the club in hand, go across with a spade and lead a diamond. If a first-round finesse loses and the clubs are cleared, you will then need fast tricks. So you will test for a doubleton heart queen before playing diamonds again.

Of course East may have long clubs and the eight does look more like a lead from small cards than a fourth highest. If East has five clubs and your stopper goes at trick one, West needs only one diamond honour to regain the lead. You risk losing four clubs and a diamond. Do you want to try ducking the club in both hands? Then you will go down when your left-hand opponent started with three clubs and both diamond honours.

To cut out East's clubs you should call for the queen at trick one. The ace wins, but you duck the second club and win the third. This exhausts West of clubs. Going up with the queen does not harm your chances if the lead is fourth best after all. As East can never get in, you will still have two stoppers. It is also unlikely that a heart switch at trick two will cause problems.

***Work out which defender you will expect to lose the lead to – it may affect your play at trick one.***

Example 58

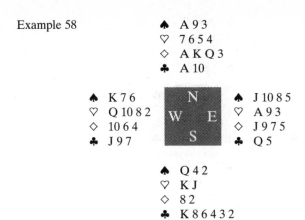

                    ♠ A 9 3
                    ♡ 7 6 5 4
                    ◇ A K Q 3
                    ♣ A 10

  ♠ K 7 6                          ♠ J 10 8 5
  ♡ Q 10 8 2                       ♡ A 9 3
  ◇ 10 6 4                         ◇ J 9 7 5
  ♣ J 9 7                          ♣ Q 5

                    ♠ Q 4 2
                    ♡ K J
                    ◇ 8 2
                    ♣ K 8 6 4 3 2

Yet again you declare the no-trump game. West leads the two of hearts and East wins with the ace, returning the nine (a low one back would prove more effective for the defence).

With one heart in the bag you can reckon on seven sure tricks – two in the majors, three diamonds and two clubs. The queen of spades offers scope for only one extra winner, which means you must develop the clubs. Prospects appear bleak if they do not break 3-2; hence we assume they do.

Although the heart attack has saved you a guess, it has removed an entry to your long suit. Furthermore it has put the defenders in a position to cash two more heart tricks whenever one of them gains the lead. West's lead of the two and East's high return mark the suit's layout as shown in the diagram.

Do you see what will happen if you simply play three rounds of clubs? The defence will make a club trick plus their hearts, giving them four in all. After taking the diamond exit, you cannot lead up to the spade queen since the king would be the setting trick. Unless the king falls under the ace, you will go down.

Before conceding a club you should cash three rounds of diamonds. You hope West wins the club and cannot lead the three of hearts to East's eight. You also need to find the ♠K on your left and the long diamonds on your right. Happily your luck holds. Having cashed the hearts, West exits with a spade, which gives you the queen and access to your remaining club.

*When you can ill afford to lose an extra trick, do not rely on a slow winner providing an entry.*

Example 59

Love All
Dealer South

♠ J 9 5 4
♡ A 5
◇ A K J 8
♣ Q 9 2

| SOUTH | WEST | NORTH | EAST |
|-------|------|-------|------|
| 1NT | Pass | 2♣ | Pass |
| 2◇ | Pass | 3NT | End |

♠ K Q 6
♡ J 7
◇ 7 5 3 2
♣ A K 7 3

West leads the two of hearts and East puts up the king when you duck in dummy. The four of hearts comes back, knocking out your only stopper in the suit.

Faced with the need to run nine tricks without losing the lead, how do you set about your task?

Example 60

East–West game
Dealer South

♠ 7 4
♡ 10 9 6 5
◇ A Q
♣ K 7 6 4 2

| SOUTH | WEST | NORTH | EAST |
|-------|------|-------|------|
| 1♡ | Pass | 3♡ | Pass |
| 4♡ | All Pass | | |

♠ K Q 5
♡ A 7 4 3 2
◇ K 9
♣ A J 5

West leads the three of spades to East's ace. You capture the two of spades return with your king.

Your likely problem is to avoid losing two trumps and a club in addition to the spade already lost. How do you address this?

Example 61

Game All
Dealer East

♠ A J 8
♥ 9 8 5 4
♦ 3 2
♣ Q J 5 3

| SOUTH | WEST | NORTH | EAST |
|-------|------|-------|------|
|       |      |       | 1♦   |
| 1♥    | 1♠*  | 3♥**  | Pass |
| 4♥    | All Pass |   |      |

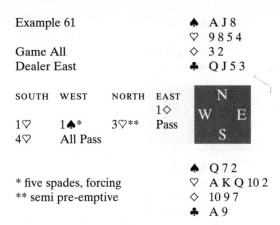

* five spades, forcing
** semi pre-emptive

♠ Q 7 2
♥ A K Q 10 2
♦ 10 9 7
♣ A 9

West leads the king of diamonds and continues with the six to East's jack. The ace of diamonds comes back next and you are grateful to see a small spade appearing on your left.

How do you plan the play from here?

Example 62

Love All
Dealer East

♠ A J 7 5
♥ K 8 5 3 2
♦ J 8 2
♣ 10

| SOUTH | WEST | NORTH | EAST |
|-------|------|-------|------|
|       |      |       | 1♣   |
| 1♥    | Dbl* | 4♥    | End  |

* negative, four spades

♠ K 9 2
♥ A Q 7 6 4
♦ K 6 3
♣ J 7

West leads the two of clubs to the ace. East switches to the jack of trumps.

How do you approach this hand?

Example 59

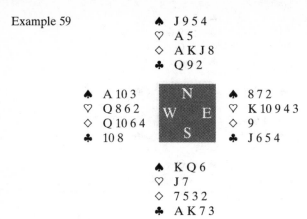

```
            ♠ J 9 5 4
            ♡ A 5
            ◇ A K J 8
            ♣ Q 9 2

♠ A 10 3                    ♠ 8 7 2
♡ Q 8 6 2        N         ♡ K 10 9 4 3
◇ Q 10 6 4     W   E       ◇ 9
♣ 10 8           S         ♣ J 6 5 4

            ♠ K Q 6
            ♡ J 7
            ◇ 7 5 3 2
            ♣ A K 7 3
```

With East-West silent you reach 3NT. West leads the two of hearts and dummy's ace wins the second round of the suit.

Barring a surprise heart blockage you have no time to play spades and you will require four tricks apiece from the minors.

In clubs a 3-3 division offers your main chance. An honour might fall on your left under the queen, but you must not go on to take a double finesse. West can freely drop a high card from ♣J-10-x. Since you lack a re-entry to hand, jack-ten alone with East will not help either. On the other hand, provided you avoid blocking the suit, you can handle such a holding with West. Next time around you lead the *nine* to the ace. Then when you get back to dummy, you can finesse the seven. This works too if West has ♣10-8 or ♣J-8 and only loses out to ♣J-10-8.

No doubt you should start diamonds with the ace. If East follows with the queen, you can then lead twice through West's ten-nine. This means you must attack diamonds before playing a second round of clubs. East's first diamond is in fact the nine. It might be from ten-nine bare, but it is twice as likely to be a singleton – this is a standard restricted choice position. Here you need not worry about East fooling around with ◇10-9-x; in that case West's queen pops up on the second round. So you use your two club entries to finesse firstly the eight and then the jack of diamonds. Happily all passes off peacefully. Phew!

***When a fairly high card falls on the first round of a suit it is often right to take a deep finesse next time.***

Example 60

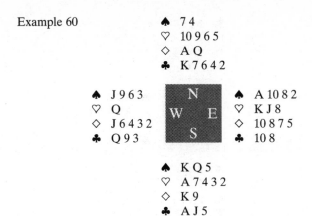

```
                    ♠ 7 4
                    ♡ 10 9 6 5
                    ◇ A Q
                    ♣ K 7 6 4 2

   ♠ J 9 6 3         N          ♠ A 10 8 2
   ♡ Q          W         E      ♡ K J 8
   ◇ J 6 4 3 2                   ◇ 10 8 7 5
   ♣ Q 9 3           S          ♣ 10 8

                    ♠ K Q 5
                    ♡ A 7 4 3 2
                    ◇ K 9
                    ♣ A J 5
```

You play in 4♡ with no opposing bidding. West leads the three of spades to the ace and your king wins the ♠2 return.

A 2-2 trump split makes the contract a cinch and on a 4-0 break only an inspired trump endplay would work (give West a 4-4-2-3 shape but no ♣Q). Thus you focus on the 3-1 layouts.

If you have to give the defence two trump tricks, you must avoid conceding a club. For sure you could cash the king and finesse East for the queen, but can you spot something better?

By cashing some side-suit winners before letting the enemy score their trump winners, you might secure a helpful return. Indeed if West holds the trump length you can guarantee the contract. After cashing the ♡A, take your boss spade and two diamonds before giving the defence their hearts. A club return allows a free finesse whilst a ruff discard suits you equally well.

In fact West drops the queen under the ♡A, East producing the eight. Again the odds heavily favour the queen being the singleton: while a player dealt honour-honour-eight must follow low, someone with K-Q-J could play any of these three cards.

Placing East with three trumps you reassess your strategy. The other defender, who you assume has two fewer hearts, figures to hold longer clubs and of course the ♣Q. So cash your side winners, finishing with a club to the king and one back to the ace. Then you exit with a heart. East will have to lead a pointed suit, allowing you to ruff in dummy and discard a club.

***Sometimes the fall of a spot card provides a major clue on how the suit is breaking.***

Example 61

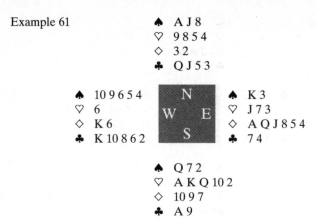

&spades; A J 8
&hearts; 9 8 5 4
&diams; 3 2
&clubs; Q J 5 3

&spades; 10 9 6 5 4     &spades; K 3
&hearts; 6     &hearts; J 7 3
&diams; K 6     &diams; A Q J 8 5 4
&clubs; K 10 8 6 2     &clubs; 7 4

&spades; Q 7 2
&hearts; A K Q 10 2
&diams; 10 9 7
&clubs; A 9

Once more you are in Four Hearts. This time diamonds have been bid on your right and spades on your left. West leads from king other diamond and the defence plays three rounds of the suit. Happily for you, West does not produce the jack of trumps.

You start by ruffing the third trick in dummy. Before drawing trumps you check whether you might want to use this entry.

You can afford to lose one black-suit trick and may wonder which finesse to take first. If you run the club queen and West turns up with the king, you establish the jack. This allows you to discard one spade, after which the spade finesse would see you home. Taking the spade finesse and then the club finesse comes to the same thing. You need one out of the two to work.

Now think back to the bidding. East's 1&diams; opener and West's response coupled with what has happened in diamonds ought to tell you one thing. The black kings will be in opposite hands. Whenever one king sits over an ace, so will the other.

If the &clubs;K turns up on your left, you could try to drop the &spades;K offside, but there is a much better line. Draw trumps and lead ace followed by another club. If West rises with the king, you have two discards for your spades. If the defender ducks, you do not lose a club. You would get home too if East holds the club king. The spade finesse would become a sure thing and dummy's other club honour would take care of your third spade.

*Before leading an honour for a finesse, first consider whether playing up to it could work better.*

Example 62

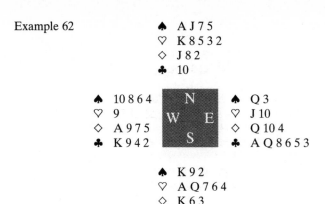

```
            ♠  A J 7 5
            ♡  K 8 5 3 2
            ◇  J 8 2
            ♣  10

  ♠  10 8 6 4              ♠  Q 3
  ♡  9                     ♡  J 10
  ◇  A 9 7 5               ◇  Q 10 4
  ♣  K 9 4 2               ♣  A Q 8 6 5 3

            ♠  K 9 2
            ♡  A Q 7 6 4
            ◇  K 6 3
            ♣  J 7
```

A trio of heart games completes its run. East opened 1♣ as dealer and West has shown four spades with a few values. The defence starts with a club to the ace and the heart jack switch.

As a start you can safely draw trumps ending in hand and ruff a club in dummy. After that you should decide how best to restrict your losers in spades and diamonds to at most two.

It looks like you are bound to lose two diamond tricks, which rather suggests you must bring in the spades without loss. If so, you need to assume the ace of diamonds sits on your right and the queen of spades is on your left.

Now wait a minute. Once you place the diamond ace onside the king gives second-round control in the suit. This means any three spade tricks will suffice because a discard will be useful.

With the spades marked as 4-2 on the bidding you can make sure of three winners in the suit. Cash the ace, come back to the king and lead towards the jack. If West turns up with queen to four, you can relax. East surely needs the diamond ace to justify the opening bid. You just lose one trick in each side suit.

A bonus arises when East holds the spade queen. She falls on the second round, allowing you to take three fast spade winners. You continue by playing a fourth round, throwing away a low diamond. Upon winning this trick, West must concede a ruff and discard or lead up to your king of diamonds.

**If a lower honour is useful whenever it wins a trick, you may be able to cater for a short honour offside.**

Example 63

Game All
Dealer South

♠ A J
♡ K 7 3
◇ A K Q 7 2
♣ A J 10

| SOUTH | WEST | NORTH | EAST |
|-------|------|-------|------|
| 3♠ | Pass | 4NT | Pass |
| 5◇* | Pass | 6♠ | End |

N
W    E
S

* one key card

♠ K Q 10 9 8 6 5
♡ 10 6 5
◇ —
♣ 8 5 3

Partner could have checked for the trump queen by bidding 5♡ over 5◇. However such an enquiry would have risked East doubling for a heart lead; besides, your vulnerable pre-empt was likely to be based on a good suit.

Plan the play on the lead of the four of diamonds.

Example 64

Love All
Dealer South

♠ 8 6 5 2
♡ Q 4 3
◇ A J 3
♣ Q 6 3

| SOUTH | WEST | NORTH | EAST |
|-------|------|-------|------|
| 1◇ | 2♡* | Double | 3♡** |
| 4♣ | Pass | 4◇ | End |

N
W    E
S

* weak
** not a try for game

♠ A K
♡ 9
◇ K Q 10 9 2
♣ K 8 5 4 2

West cashes the ace of hearts, East playing the five, and then leads the three of spades to East's jack and your ace.

How should you handle this part-score?

Example 65
♠ A 7 4 3
♡ Q J 10
Game All
♦ Q 5
Dealer West
♣ A K Q 9

| SOUTH | WEST | NORTH | EAST |
|-------|------|-------|------|
|       | Pass | 1♣    | Pass |
| 1♡    | Double | Rdbl | Pass |
| Pass  | 2♦   | 2♡    | Pass |
| 2NT   | Pass | 3NT   | End  |

♠ K J
♡ 9 8 6 3
♦ A 9 8
♣ J 10 7 3

Partner's redouble of the take-out showed general values.

West tables the six of diamonds against your 3NT. Dummy's queen holds and East follows with the two, suggesting an odd number of cards in the suit.

What line offers your best chance?

Example 66
♠ 6 2
♡ A K 8 6 5 3
North–South game
♦ 7 5
Dealer North
♣ A K 10

| SOUTH | WEST | NORTH | EAST |
|-------|------|-------|------|
|       |      | 1♡    | Pass |
| 3♦    | 3♠   | Pass  | Pass |
| 3NT   | Pass | 4♡*   | Pass |
| 4♠**  | Pass | 5♣**  | Pass |
| 6♦    | All Pass |   |      |

* forward going
**cue bid

♠ A Q 8
♡ 7 4
♦ A K Q J 10 4
♣ 7 2

West hits upon the eight of clubs for the opening lead.

What strategy do you adopt on this hand?

Example 63

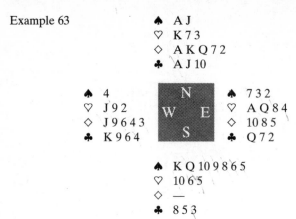

```
              ♠ A J
              ♡ K 7 3
              ◇ A K Q 7 2
              ♣ A J 10

♠ 4                        ♠ 7 3 2
♡ J 9 2                    ♡ A Q 8 4
◇ J 9 6 4 3                ◇ 10 8 5
♣ K 9 6 4                  ♣ Q 7 2

              ♠ K Q 10 9 8 6 5
              ♡ 10 6 5
              ◇ —
              ♣ 8 5 3
```

You are playing in Six Spades after a smooth auction. West leads the four of diamonds.

You can see eleven easy winners – seven trumps, three diamonds and the club ace. Sources of a twelfth include the heart king (if you try testing West for the ace), a long diamond (if they break 4-4 and you ruff one) and the double club finesse.

You have two decisions to make. Firstly, do you throw hearts or clubs on the diamond tops? Secondly, when do you do so?

Assuming West would have preferred to lead from ♣K-Q rather than a weak diamond suit, a two in three chance exists of finding a club honour on your left. On the other hand, playing for the ace of hearts to lie onside represents a mere 50-50 shot. Therefore you intend to discard three hearts on the diamonds.

You could ruff the opening lead and attempt to draw trumps ending in dummy. If the spades are 2-2, you can safely test the diamonds and ruff a red card to hand if they fail to behave. Sadly a snag arises on a 3-1 trump split. You cannot quickly get back to hand to pull the last trump. This means leading the boss diamonds with a trump still out. As you might expect, the third trump lies with the short diamonds and a ruff beats you.

You do better to win trick one in dummy and take two rounds of trumps straight away. Then take two more diamond winners before ruffing a low one. Now only a 6-2 or 7-1 diamond break will upset you, both of which sound unlikely given the ◇4 lead.

*Cashing early the high cards in a suit you want to ruff can work well when you cannot readily draw trumps.*

Example 64

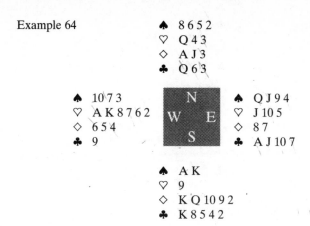

```
                    ♠ 8 6 5 2
                    ♡ Q 4 3
                    ◇ A J 3
                    ♣ Q 6 3

    ♠ 10 7 3               ♠ Q J 9 4
    ♡ A K 8 7 6 2     N    ♡ J 10 5
    ◇ 6 5 4        W     E ◇ 8 7
    ♣ 9               S    ♣ A J 10 7

                    ♠ A K
                    ♡ 9
                    ◇ K Q 10 9 2
                    ♣ K 8 5 4 2
```

For a change you are in 4◇. West leads the ace of hearts and switches to the spade three, East's jack drawing your ace.

Ten tricks are easy if both minors split 3-2: just draw trumps and set up the clubs. How might you counter the 4-1 breaks?

For a start you do not want to lead a club to the queen early on. As the bidding suggests East holds the ♣A, that is the suit more likely to break 4-1. After topping the queen with the ace, East can return a high club to allow West to ruff out your king.

A low club to the king seems better. However, that entails using a trump entry to dummy, which means you must put West with three trumps (else East can draw North's). You must also take care to cash the king of spades before anyone can ruff it.

That play works on the actual lie but would fail if East had four diamonds and three clubs. East would win the second club and punch you with a heart. Then you would run out of trumps.

You might seek to guard against the heart force by leading a club to the eight. Of course East may have ace-ten-nine or better and, in any event, that line is useless if clubs break 4-1.

By far the best way to tackle the clubs is to lay down the king. You are cold with them 3-2 (and trumps 4-1) since you can accept two heart forces and ruff your two long clubs high in dummy. If it is clubs 4-1, West can only ruff a loser as you will play towards the queen. True you might need to guess how many trumps to draw, but the fall of the spades may guide you.

*Stop before tackling a suit in an obvious way – the rest of the hand may make another way of handling it better.*

Example 65

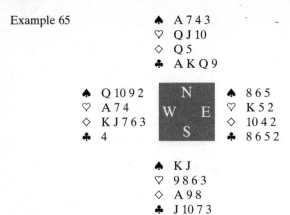

♠ A 7 4 3
♡ Q J 10
♢ Q 5
♣ A K Q 9

♠ Q 10 9 2         ♠ 8 6 5
♡ A 7 4           ♡ K 5 2
♢ K J 7 6 3      ♢ 10 4 2
♣ 4             ♣ 8 6 5 2

♠ K J
♡ 9 8 6 3
♢ A 9 8
♣ J 10 7 3

West, who passed as dealer and showed a take-out of the rounded suits with longer diamonds, leads the ♢6 against 3NT. East plays the ♢2 under the queen, implying an odd number.

Having made the queen of diamonds, you can count eight certain tricks. Given time you can establish two heart winners and the spade suit offers a finesse position. What is best?

From the bidding and play to trick one, you can foresee troubled waters if you go all out to develop heart winners. East will probably win the first round of hearts and carry on with diamonds. Holding up your ace will serve little purpose and, when you revert to hearts, West will get in and cash enough diamonds to beat you.

Sure, the hearts could break 1-5, in which case you will be able to remove West's entry first. Sadly the odds point against this. Also East may misdefend, but you would hardly wish to rely on that either. You could fall back on the spade finesse if the first round of hearts does not go the way you want it to. However, once a high heart honour turns up on your right, the bidding surely marks the queen of spades on your left.

Running your long suit sometimes saves the day. Alas, if you rattle off four rounds of clubs, West can discard two spades trusting East to take charge of North's seven. Do you give up?

In fact a line exists that, assuming West began with exactly four spades and five diamonds, guarantees success!

You should indeed put that defender under pressure with discards, but you must do so in precisely the right way.

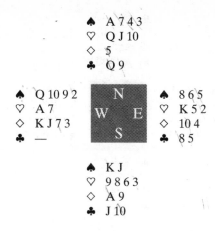

♠ A 7 4 3
♡ Q J 10
◇ 5
♣ Q 9

♠ Q 10 9 2          ♠ 8 6 5
♡ A 7          ♡ K 5 2
◇ K J 7 3          ◇ 10 4
♣ —          ♣ 8 5

♠ K J
♡ 9 8 6 3
◇ A 9
♣ J 10

In the early play you need to leave the hearts well alone. Instead, on the second and third tricks, cash a pair of top clubs. This leaves the position shown with the lead on the table. Now watch West squirm as you lead a club to the jack . . .

Releasing a diamond clearly fails. After that you can afford to attack hearts, losing just two tricks in each red suit.

Neither does a heart discard work. In that case you can again play on hearts since this will remove West's entry. Then holding up the ace of diamonds will complete the job (or you may make your victim lead from the ♠Q if you feel so inclined).

Perhaps you would like to suppose West throws a spade?

From the take-out double you can surely infer West began with four spades. Now one of them has gone, dummy has a spade more than either defender. You still possess a diamond stopper (which explains why you had to play clubs without touching hearts) and dummy has a late entry (the ♣Q, hence the low club at trick four). Thus you can play king, ace and a third spade to set up and later enjoy your ninth winner.

Note that it matters not where the major suit honours lie or if you catch a slightly different shape on your left. Being reduced to nine cards, West cannot keep four spades, four diamonds and two hearts.

***Knowing defenders often want to take their winners in a certain order, look out for ways of frustrating them.***

Example 66

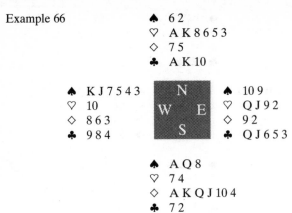

♠ 6 2
♡ A K 8 6 5 3
♢ 7 5
♣ A K 10

♠ K J 7 5 4 3
♡ 10
♢ 8 6 3
♣ 9 8 4

♠ 10 9
♡ Q J 9 2
♢ 9 2
♣ Q J 6 5 3

♠ A Q 8
♡ 7 4
♢ A K Q J 10 4
♣ 7 2

After West has put in a cheeky Three Spade overcall you are at the helm in Six Diamonds. The lead is the eight of clubs.

You could have done without the club lead, which you have to win with dummy's ace. With both the outside entries to the hearts intact, you would have managed to ruff twice and run the suit even on a 4-1 break. Even as things stand, a 3-2 break will allow you to ruff the suit good and record an overtrick.

West's spade bid warns that East may be able to overruff the third round of spades. This factor, coupled with the attractive prospects in hearts, tells you to forget about ruffing a spade in dummy. Therefore you draw trumps.

All follow to the first two rounds and West follows to the third one as well. On this trick you take great care to pitch a heart from dummy, for reasons that will become apparent later. East discards a club.

Although double dummy there are other ways to succeed, the natural line is to test the hearts next. You cash the ace-king but West throws a spade. You hardly fancy the spade finesse, but chances of a throw-in at the end look good. Unless East has ♠J-(x)-(x) or ♠10-(x)-(x) and rises with an honour on the first round of the suit, the contract can be made.

In order to finish leading your trumps, you ruff a heart back to hand, and West again sheds a spade. On your fifth diamond this defender throws another spade, while to conserve North's black cards, a heart goes from dummy.

Now see the position at the point you lead your final trump:

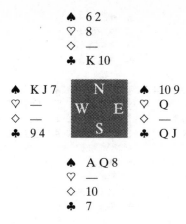

♠ 6 2
♡ 8
◇ —
♣ K 10

♠ K J 7            ♠ 10 9
♡ —               ♡ Q
◇ —               ◇ —
♣ 9 4             ♣ Q J

♠ A Q 8
♡ —
◇ 10
♣ 7

On the ◇10 West has to let a club go; else you make a long spade. You would throw a heart or a club from dummy and then advance the spade queen. That way you both retain an entry to your hand and keep East, who has a master heart, off play.

Once West has trimmed down to one club you dispense with North's second low spade. As the cards lie, East too feels the pinch. The picture cards serve to stop dummy's club ten and heart eight scoring. So that defender throws the spade nine.

Now you cross to the king of clubs, stripping West's exit card in the process, and lead a spade. When the ten appears, you cover with the queen and West wins the king. Your ace and eight of spades collect the last two tricks.

Note that the endplay would work much the same if West started with ♠K-J-10-9-(x)-(x). East would stay out of the frame and you could easily duck a spade to West at trick eleven.

Note also that if West was dealt ♠K-J-10-x etc., and East the ♠9, a one-suit squeeze would see you home. If West kept three honours, you would duck the first spade. If West saved a small one, you could afford to top the nine with the queen.

The actual sequence of plays, in which East's discard made your ace-queen-eight good enough to force an endplay, was a mole squeeze.

*If your spot cards may not be quite good enough for an endplay, try the effect of running your long suit.*

Example 67

|  | | | | ♠ | A 10 |
|---|---|---|---|---|---|

♠ A 10
♡ K 3

North–South game
Dealer East

♢ A K 8 5 3 2
♣ Q 6 3

| SOUTH | WEST | NORTH | EAST |
|-------|------|-------|------|
|       |      |       | Pass |
| 2♡    | Pass | 4♡    | End  |

```
        N
    W       E
        S
```

♠ J
♡ A Q J 10 4 2
♢ J 4
♣ 8 7 5 2

West leads the nine of clubs. East overtakes with the ten and shifts to the four of spades. This goes jack, king, ace.

With the side entry to dummy's diamonds gone, what can you do about your fourth-round club loser?

Example 68

♠ Q 10 5 4
♡ A 8 4

East–West game
Dealer West

♢ 6 5 4
♣ A 10 4

| SOUTH | WEST | NORTH | EAST |
|-------|------|-------|------|
|       | 1♡   | Pass  | 3♡   |
| 3♠    | Pass | 4♠    | End  |

```
        N
    W       E
        S
```

♠ A K 9 8 6 3
♡ —
♢ Q 8 3 2
♣ Q 7 6

West selects the seven of hearts for the opening lead.
How do you aim to limit your minor-suit losers to three?

Example 69

East–West game
Dealer East

♠ A 10 5 4
♡ Q 10 9
◇ A J 5
♣ K 7 3

| SOUTH | WEST | NORTH | EAST |
|-------|------|-------|------|
|       |      |       | 1◇   |
| 1♡    | 1♠   | 2◇*   | Pass |
| 2♡    | 2♠   | Double| Pass |
| 4♡    | All Pass | | |

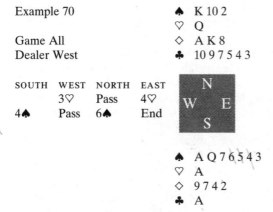

* value raise

♠ 7
♡ A K J 6 5 4
◇ 8 6 2
♣ Q 8 5

West leads the nine of East's suit, diamonds.
How can you give yourself a decent shot for this contract?

Example 70

Game All
Dealer West

♠ K 10 2
♡ Q
◇ A K 8
♣ 10 9 7 5 4 3

| SOUTH | WEST | NORTH | EAST |
|-------|------|-------|------|
|       | 3♡   | Pass  | 4♡   |
| 4♠    | Pass | 6♠    | End  |

♠ A Q 7 6 5 4 3
♡ A
◇ 9 7 4 2
♣ A

West leads the seven of hearts, which goes queen, nine, ace. Perhaps planning to claim, you lay down the trump ace. West dispels any such thoughts by discarding a small heart.

How do you respond to this?

Example 67

&spades; A 10
&hearts; K 3
&diams; A K 8 5 3 2
&clubs; Q 6 3

&spades; K 8 7 5 2      N      &spades; Q 9 6 4 3
&hearts; 8 6 5     W   E   &hearts; 9 7
&diams; Q 9 7       S     &diams; 10 6
&clubs; 9 4          &clubs; A K J 10

&spades; J
&hearts; A Q J 10 4 2
&diams; J 4
&clubs; 8 7 5 2

After you open Two Hearts in second seat partner puts you to four. West leads the nine of clubs to East's ten and the four of spades comes back. The king and ace cover your jack.

From the way the first trick has gone, you conclude that West has led with a doubleton or singleton club. This indicates you cannot set up a long club winner.

Prospects for ruffing a club seem poor as East can shift to a trump when next in. Even if the hearts split 1-4, you still cannot engineer a ruff since West can ruff the third round of clubs to continue trumps. Despite this, attacking clubs could work. You will set up a simple squeeze if one opponent holds length in both minors. Can you see anything better?

Playing a second round of clubs will not only oblige East to attack trumps but it will also cut the link between the two defenders. If you can then arrange to develop a diamond trick without letting East back in, you can throw a club on a diamond. If West has the queen of diamonds and the suit breaks 3-2, that is a piece of cake. After making the club play, draw trumps and lead the jack of diamonds, ducking in dummy.

Remember East passed as dealer and has showed up with the ace-king-jack of clubs. You can infer the spade queen sits on your right as well: West might have led from king-queen of spades at trick one or played the lower of touching honours at trick two. Clearly the avoidance play must be the correct line.

***Chances to cut the link between the defenders can take many forms – watch out for ways of using them.***

Example 68

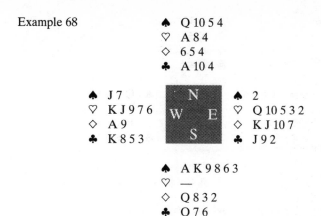

```
              ♠ Q 10 5 4
              ♡ A 8 4
              ◇ 6 5 4
              ♣ A 10 4

  ♠ J 7                      ♠ 2
  ♡ K J 9 7 6      N         ♡ Q 10 5 3 2
  ◇ A 9          W   E       ◇ K J 10 7
  ♣ K 8 5 3        S         ♣ J 9 2

              ♠ A K 9 8 6 3
              ♡ —
              ◇ Q 8 3 2
              ♣ Q 7 6
```

West, who opened 1♡ and heard East give a jump raise, leads the seven of the suit against your Four Spade contract.

You will discard one club on the ace of hearts, which means you face four possible losers: three diamonds and a club.

With West having an opening bid (and East marked with something in hearts on the lead) the likelihood of finding ◇A-K on your right is very slim. West might have a bare ace or king, but really you have to reckon on losing three diamonds.

Unless West's ♣K is single, you cannot tackle clubs without loss. Moreover, one discard on any long diamond will not help with a second-round club loser. Well, what plan could work?

You conclude that you should aim to compel the defence to attack clubs or concede a ruff and discard. The odds are, that in the process of stripping diamonds, each defender will get the chance to lead clubs. So your best hope is to find a frozen club suit i.e., putting the king on your left and the jack on your right.

Win with the ♡A, discarding a club, ruff a heart, draw trumps ending in dummy and ruff another heart. Next do not cross to dummy with a third trump to lead a diamond up to your queen. As the cards lie West can win with the ace and exit with the nine, allowing East to play two more rounds. Instead simply duck a diamond. Barring West having ◇A-K-x-x (a most unlikely holding given the choice of opening lead), the defence will have to open up the clubs. You then duck if a low club is led from either side.

*A frozen suit confers a great benefit and you ought to strive to take full advantage of it.*

Example 69

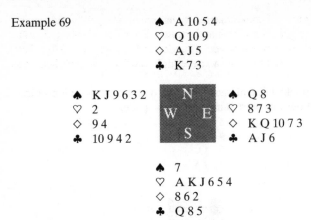

&spades; A 10 5 4
&hearts; Q 10 9
&diams; A J 5
&clubs; K 7 3

&spades; K J 9 6 3 2     &spades; Q 8
&hearts; 2     &hearts; 8 7 3
&diams; 9 4     &diams; K Q 10 7 3
&clubs; 10 9 4 2     &clubs; A J 6

&spades; 7
&hearts; A K J 6 5 4
&diams; 8 6 2
&clubs; Q 8 5

Although 3NT by North would prove much easier, you have found your way into 4♡. West leads the nine of diamonds.

You can locate nine easy winners but the tenth may escape you for a minute. On the bidding you can expect to find the ♣A on your right, but there is no reason why it should be doubleton.

To make both your king and queen of clubs you will have to arrange for East to lead the suit. You intend to throw East in with a diamond and, provided this player has no safe exit cards, you will obtain the desired club return.

If trumps divide evenly, you can strip the hand without too much trouble. You ruff a spade or two in hand, draw trumps and cut loose with a diamond. East can score two diamond winners (you won the first trick lest West had led a singleton) but must then lead a club or give a ruff and discard.

As you can see from the diagram, East does in fact have three trumps and the endplay described above fails. In order to extract East's third trump you need to play a third round of hearts, which means your opponent can exit with a diamond.

A possible strip squeeze may come to mind. Sadly that goes awry for a slightly different reason. East maintains parity with your club length until the last trump lead and only then releases a club. You cannot derive any advantage from the shortened ace of clubs because the defender has a long diamond to cash.

Putting pressure on East's hand indeed provides the answer – the correct way comes through ruffing three spades in hand.

Dummy contains limited entries, so having gone up with the ace of diamonds, you lead a low club at trick two. Poor East ducks and your queen wins. You cross to the ace of spades and ruff a spade. After that play a trump to dummy, ruff a spade high and lead another heart to dummy.

East has pitched one diamond and the diagram shows the position as you are about to trump dummy's fourth spade:

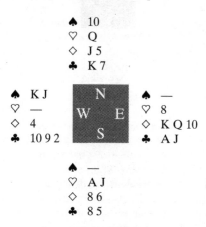

```
                    ♠   10
                    ♡   Q
                    ◇   J 5
                    ♣   K 7

    ♠   K J              N              ♠   —
    ♡   —                               ♡   8
    ◇   4            W       E          ◇   K Q 10
    ♣   10 9 2           S              ♣   A J

                    ♠   —
                    ♡   A J
                    ◇   8 6
                    ♣   8 5
```

For sure East cannot throw a club on the ten of spades, or else at trick nine you can knock out the ace with a low card. Neither does ruffing profit the defence. You overruff and have achieved the objective of drawing trumps whilst leaving one in dummy. In that case it is just as if the trumps were 2-2 all the time and you can exit with a diamond.

Suppose then East discards a diamond. Now you ruff with the jack, pull the last trump and lead a diamond to the jack. East wins two diamonds but must play a club at trick twelve.

Note that the dummy reversal did not gain you any trump tricks. You started with and ended up with six. However it provided the only safe way to get rid of East's long diamond. Geza Ottlik named this class of technique a knockout squeeze. You can read more about such positions in *Adventures in Card Play*, which he co-wrote with Hugh Kelsey. It remains in print.

*On occasion ruffing in the long hand can bring pressure to bear on an opponent with a trump left.*

Example 70

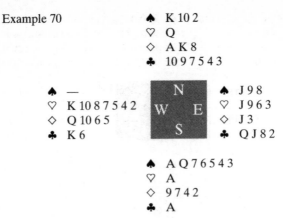

&spades; K 10 2
&hearts; Q
&diams; A K 8
&clubs; 10 9 7 5 4 3

&spades; —
&hearts; K 10 8 7 5 4 2
&diams; Q 10 6 5
&clubs; K 6

&spades; J 9 8
&hearts; J 9 6 3
&diams; J 3
&clubs; Q J 8 2

&spades; A Q 7 6 5 4 3
&hearts; A
&diams; 9 7 4 2
&clubs; A

After East has raised West's pre-empt in hearts to game, you bounce into a small slam in spades. The initial lead looks like a fourth-best heart and your ace wins. At trick two you lay down the ace of trumps, but West shows out, pitching a heart.

You could still play to trump a possible fourth-round diamond loser in dummy as East may well have the defence's diamond length. After all, the 0-3 spade split merely balances out the expected 7-4 heart layout. What else might you try?

On the table there is a long club suit and three entries. So if the unseen clubs divide three apiece, you can establish the suit with a couple of ruffs, cash the &spades;Q and get back to enjoy it.

Surely you ought to aim to combine your chances. At the third trick unblock the ace of clubs, then go across to the deck with a diamond and ruff a club.

You could now go back to dummy's second high diamond and trump another club. You would be okay if the clubs broke or if West had the length (then East would have three or more diamonds). As the cards lie though, that play brings defeat.

To succeed, you should indeed lead a second diamond, but play dummy's eight (West cannot afford to split honours). East wins and faces only losing options. A heart is clearly out and a club return gives you the extra entry needed to ruff out the suit. A trump into the king-ten produces the same result. If East did have another diamond to exit with then either the suit is breaking or a ruff is possible.

*If you appear to be one entry short, try enlisting the help of an opponent.*

Example 71         ♠ K 9 4
                     ♡ A Q 7 3

Love All         ♦ K 7 6 4
Dealer East     ♣ A Q

| SOUTH | WEST | NORTH | EAST |
|-------|------|-------|------|
|  |  |  | 1NT |
| Pass | 2◊* | Double | Pass** |
| 3♣ | Pass | 3NT | Pass |
| 4♠ | All Pass |  |  |

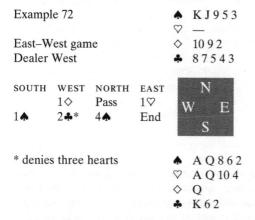

                   ♠ Q 7 6 5 2

\* transfer              ♡ 10 2
\*\* denies three hearts  ♦ —
                   ♣ K J 10 8 4 3

Partner's double showed a hand that would have doubled East's 12-14 1NT. Your 3♣ bid was forcing.

West leads the ◊Q, which you duck in dummy and ruff in hand. You advance the ♠5, which goes three, king, ace. East plays back the ♠J to your queen, West discarding a low heart.

Can you find a way to avoid losing a heart?

Example 72         ♠ K J 9 5 3
                     ♡ —
East–West game  ♦ 10 9 2
Dealer West    ♣ 8 7 5 4 3

| SOUTH | WEST | NORTH | EAST |
|-------|------|-------|------|
|  | 1◊ | Pass | 1♡ |
| 1♠ | 2♣* | 4♠ | End |

\* denies three hearts  ♠ A Q 8 6 2
                   ♡ A Q 10 4
                   ♦ Q
                   ♣ K 6 2

West leads the ace of diamonds and East follows with the six. After studying the fall of the diamonds, West switches to a small trump.

How can you cater for the ace of clubs being on your left?

Example 71

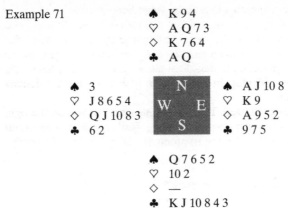

```
              ♠ K 9 4
              ♡ A Q 7 3
              ◇ K 7 6 4
              ♣ A Q

♠ 3                         ♠ A J 10 8
♡ J 8 6 5 4      N          ♡ K 9
◇ Q J 10 8 3   W   E        ◇ A 9 5 2
♣ 6 2            S          ♣ 9 7 5

              ♠ Q 7 6 5 2
              ♡ 10 2
              ◇ —
              ♣ K J 10 8 4 3
```

After you have heard a 12-14 1NT on your right and a transfer to hearts on your left you reach game in spades. You ruff the ◇Q opening lead and play a small trump. East tops the king with the ace and returns the jack, West pitching the ♡4.

You must lose three trump tricks, which means you need to avoid losing a heart. Of course you know the king of hearts lies on your right. The defence began with only 16 points and West has shown up with the queen-jack of diamonds. Trying to ruff a heart is hopeless – once you have pitched three hearts on the clubs, East can ruff, pull North's trump and exit to the bare ♡A.

As was the case on example 69, a lead from East could prove helpful, but the player in question holds too many trumps for your liking. If you merely cash enough rounds of clubs to extract East's and exit with a spade, the defender will draw your other trump and cash the ace of diamonds. Furthermore, you would lack a route back to whatever clubs remain in your hand.

With few other options you try running the clubs, taking the ace first and next playing the queen to the king. If East ruffs at some point, it appears your game makes. East takes a second trump but then any diamond exit permits you to score dummy's king. A heart switch is equally fatal for the enemy. Maybe East never ruffs. You still get home. Having finished the clubs you cross to the ♡A and lead a diamond off dummy to score a ruff. Is the answer really this painless?

Sorry to say, a competent East will shed two diamonds, then ruff your last club, cash the ♠10 and exit with the ace of diamonds – you see dummy's king will have lost its guard by this time.

Suppose you trump that final club – what happens then?

Your opponent overruffs, cashes the other trump winner and dummy is squeezed just the same. Only three tricks come after this one, which means you cannot retain ♥A-Q and ◇K-x on the table. In addition to the ace of diamonds, East has king and another heart left, so can safely get off play through the suit in which you leave dummy with a singleton.

Let us go back one step. That ruffing idea has put you on the right track, but you need to improve the timing. Rather than waiting to ruff the sixth club, try the effect of trumping the fifth. Observe the result:

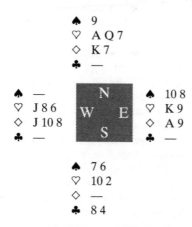

```
            ♠  9
            ♥  A Q 7
            ◇  K 7
            ♣  —

♠  —                        ♠  10 8
♥  J 8 6         N          ♥  K 9
◇  J 10 8      W   E        ◇  A 9
♣  —             S          ♣  —

            ♠  7 6
            ♥  10 2
            ◇  —
            ♣  8 4
```

For the reasons with which we are well versed, East can ill afford to overruff. Having scored the spade ten and cashed the eight, a lead of either red suit presents you with the tenth trick. On the other hand, the defender cannot escape by discarding.

If East releases a heart, you can cash the ace, felling the king, and continue with the queen . . . or you can use this chance and the ♥A re-entry to ruff two diamonds – ten tricks either way.

If a diamond is thrown instead, you lead a low diamond off dummy ruffing out the ace. After that you can lead a club or a trump. In both cases East collects two trump tricks but must concede the remainder to dummy.

*Trumping one's own winner is easily overlooked – aim to keep an open mind about such plays.*

Example 72

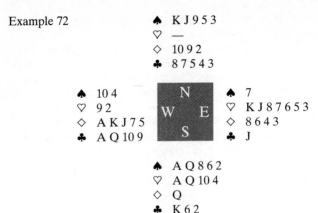

```
                    ♠ K J 9 5 3
                    ♡ —
                    ◇ 10 9 2
                    ♣ 8 7 5 4 3

  ♠ 10 4              N            ♠ 7
  ♡ 9 2          W        E        ♡ K J 8 7 6 5 3
  ◇ A K J 7 5        S            ◇ 8 6 4 3
  ♣ A Q 10 9                       ♣ J

                    ♠ A Q 8 6 2
                    ♡ A Q 10 4
                    ◇ Q
                    ♣ K 6 2
```

You are in 4♠ after West bid the minors and East hearts. West cashes the diamond ace and carefully shifts to a trump.

West's opening bid and free rebid taken with East's relative inaction on a rather shapely hand tend to mark the ace of clubs on your left. In consequence, to succeed, you will surely need to arrange some helpful leads from the defenders.

You win trick two in dummy and ruff a diamond. You go back over with a spade and trump a second diamond, after which comes a key move, ruffing the four of hearts (a slightly different order in taking these ruffs works too). Next you duck a club . . .

Given that the defence certainly do not want to lead a club up to your king, it matters not who wins this trick. Suppose for the time being that whoever wins plays back a diamond. You must ruff it in the closed hand, for yours has become the short trump hand. Also you need to secure a second friendly return – you still remain a trick short. Now you proffer the queen of hearts (this might squash the ♡J), getting rid of a second club from dummy. East wins and then has to give you a free finesse, allowing you to discard the last two clubs off the table.

If someone prefers a heart switch at trick eight, you take the queen, cash the ace (or vice versa if East plays the king) and exit with the ten. Three clubs go away from dummy on these heart tricks and a fourth does on East's forced heart return.

*When throwing the opponents in once on a deal will not suffice, see if you can find a way to endplay them twice!*